D0323781

*Impact of Renewal
on Priests & Religious*

INSTITUTE OF SPIRITUALITY

*Aquinas Institute of Philosophy & Theology*
*Harlem Avenue at Division Street, River Forest, Illinois*

VOLUME II: SPECIAL LECTURES DELIVERED IN
THE SUMMER OF 1966

*Other Volumes in the Series*:

VOLUME I: *Sex, Love, & the Life of the Spirit*

VOLUME III: *Christian Spirituality East & West*
(In preparation)

# Impact of Renewal on Priests & Religious

AUGUSTINE ROCK, O.P., EDITOR

THE PRIORY PRESS, CHICAGO, ILL.

*Revisores Ordinis*: Thomas C. Donlan, O.P., S.T.D.; Bernard O'Riley, O.P. *Imprimi potest*: Gilbert J. Graham, O.P., Provincial. *Nihil obstat*: Thomas C. Donlan, O.P., Bernard O'Riley, O.P., Censores Deputati. *Imprimatur*: Rt. Rev. Msgr. Francis W. Byrne, Vicar General, Archdiocese of Chicago, December 6, 1967.

Library of Congress Catalogue Number 68-18373
© Copyright 1968 by *The Priory Press*
1165 East 54 Place, Chicago, Illinois 60615
Manufactured in the United States of America

# Introduction

The Fathers of Vatican II insist that they were not and are not satisfied with any of the decrees of the Council. Perhaps among the least satisfactory parts of the documents of Vatican II are those relating to priests. This suspicion is somewhat substantiated by the frequency with which the Pope has spoken to and of priests, their special problems and their role in the Church.

Perhaps we middle-aged priests are more at sea than the very young, who developed with the *aggiornamento*, or the very old, who are near the end of the road. Those of us whose work and way of life have kept us close to the current literature of the sacred sciences are trying to absorb what we can and to teach, preach, and make decisions in the light of current thinking. There is much good in what we have learned from our youth, but there is much that is out of date and which we must strive to shake off. It is not easy. Even Peter had to be told three times by a voice from heaven that he should not call profane what God has made clean. After that he still had to be rebuked by Paul for reverting to a way of the past. We must not let our nostalgia stand in the way of making Christianity live for the men of our times.

Many priests are vaguely troubled as their "place" in the world seems to disappear. On the one hand they are forcefully reminded that only bishops are fully priests and directly represent Christ to the people. On the other hand they are told that all the faithful share in the priesthood of

## Introduction

Christ, and that priests must move over and let the laity take their rightful share in the apostolate.

True enough, *Lumen Gentium* (par. 10) draws a clear distinction between the common priesthood and the ministerial priesthood; yet the general drift seems to attenuate the role of the priest. Actually what is happening is that the central and truly priestly role of the ministerial priest is being focused upon and spotlighted. Yet this is a role that is essentially supernatural, "for the things that pertain to God," and does not lend itself to manmade gradations of status.

To be content as a priest today a man must perhaps be more mature than ever before, in the sense especially of facing up to reality. Since the reality of his role precisely as priest is essentially a supernatural one, he must more than ever be a man of faith quickened by charity. The power vacuums and the knowledge vacuums so often filled by the priestly caste in the past are no longer there. More and more the priest can justify his existence only as a man taken from among men for the things that pertain to God.

Often men would rather honor the priest as a scholar, an administrator, an organizer, a social worker; and often the priest is tempted to prefer to be so honored. These things are tangible, human values with which men are comfortable. There is no reason why a priest should not be any of these things, but he does not need to be a priest to be any of them nor does he need to be any of them to justify his place in the sun.

The material in this book is an attempt to look at what it means to be a priest in these post-conciliar days during which so much needs to be done: on the one hand to implement the Council and to develop along the lines the teaching Church laid down; and, on the other, to control the destructive forces, ideas, and movements which seek to impose the will, the dreams, and the ambitions of a few false prophets who find in the Council directions it never took and even some it positively rejected.

Based on lectures delivered during the 1966 session of the Institute of Spirituality for priests and brothers held at the Aquinas Institute in River Forest, Illinois, these essays have been substantially reworked by their authors, either to fill out ideas that time prevented from being explored or to take account of material which post-dates the lectures themselves.

Father Flannery is the editor of *Doctrine and Life*, published in Dublin and referred to by *Herder Correspondence* as one of the two most alive Catholic publications in Ireland. Father Corcoran is widely known for his work in psychology, especially in religious institutes for both men and women. In addition to being, along with Father Corcoran, a regular staff member of the Institute of Spirituality, for several years I have devoted a substantial part of my time to conducting retreats for priests, both diocesan and religious.

Father Flannery has done pioneer work in interpreting the Decrees of Vatican II and has edited several books of commentaries on them. Father Corcoran has deliberately, at the risk of some boredom, set down in their own words the ideas of some of the best contemporary psychologists pertinent to the formation of men for the priesthood. Those charged with the work of preparing men for the priesthood often see what needs to be done but have to sell it to bishops, provincials, and other officials who are not in close enough touch to fully appreciate the characteristics of contemporary youth or the valuable insights of modern psychology. He feels that the direct quotations will be very helpful in this regard.

These essays make no attempt to exhaust their subjects; they are merely some ideas the authors hope will be useful without exhausting their readers.

The Editor

# Contents

# PART ONE:

# Priests and Religious after Vatican II

Austin Flannery, O.P., S.T.D.

# 1: Changing with the Church

It is widely recognized that we are living in times of crisis for priests and religious. In fact, just to show how widely recognized it is let me quote from a number of recent magazine articles, statements either by, or about, the clergy and religious of different countries.

The first is from the United States, from *Life International* (July 11, 1966):

> Their garb is the familiar solemn black suit and the turned collar of the Roman Catholic priest. But their talk is of dissent and rebellion and they are impatient with what they call the archaic ways and blind authoritarianism of their Church. They are a phenomenon of the post-Vatican Council period—restless priests who have taken the ideas of Pope John XXIII and turned them into a credo for liberalizing Catholicism.

The next quotation concerns Ireland, though the writer is a Welshman, writing in England's left-wing *New Statesman and Nation* (July 1, 1966). The article is entitled "Ireland's Unfinished Revolution," and the author is Mervyn Jones. The gentle—if that is the *mot juste*?—reaction he describes certainly provides a contrast with other countries.

> Today, in the period of Catholicism stamped by the figure of John XXIII, Irish Catholics are embarrassed that their Church —which has never produced important thinkers or writers—presents a diehard appearance and that no Irish prelate plays the role of Cardinal Cushing or Cardinal Suenens. But there are certainly stirrings. Certain highly intelligent priests . . . give a strong impression of waiting for the old man to die.

In May, 1966, there was a violent clash between priests and police in Barcelona, Spain. In fact, the violence was one-sided: the police beat up the priests. The English interdenominational fortnightly, *The New Christian*, carried a report on the incident on June 30, 1966, and in the course of the report it had the following to say:

> As for Vatican II-style dialogue with diocesan priests or laymen, all these come under the heading of sheep, expected to obey like sheep, but without bleating. A caricature? No doubt. But how, say the young priests, do we banish the belief in this caricature when so many of the originals reinforce it?
>
> The young priests may go to extremes, but at least they are a great improvement on the middle-aged ones who still barge around in public as if they owned everything.

The Church in England shows an enormous gap between the *avant-garde* clergy and laity and the rest of the Church. What is more alarming than the extent of the gap, however, is the incomprehension and, at times, hostility, that exist on both sides of it. The following quotation is from the liberal Dominican monthly, *New Blackfriars* (September, 1965). It is no exaggeration to say that many of his fellow religious in England would not comprehend what the author is saying. The quotation is from an article by Fergus Kerr, O.P., entitled "Theology in a God-forsaken Epoch":

> It is no secret that there is a great deal of sickness, mental and therefore physical, among religious at the present time. It is no doubt partly that immature and unstable people are attracted to religious life in the first place: but it is also and surely above all (for immature and unstable people are attracted to marriage too!) because of the tension created by the increasing gap between the pretensions of the institutions and the real sources and occasions of personal asceticism and growth in faith and maturity (when this occurs at all).

France provides an interesting and instructive contrast with the foregoing quotations. One has the *impression*—and here one is very much open to correction by facts that have escaped one—that in France, Holland, and Germany the crisis of authority has passed, that Church ruling and Church ruled *together* face a more dangerous, though less sharply-focused, crisis, a crisis of relevance to the world in which we live. The following is from an article by Henri Holstein, "The Priests Question Themselves" ("Les Pretres S'Interrogent"), in *Etudes* (June, 1966). Father Holstein quoted a statement made by a country parish priest in France, and originally quoted in *Les Pretres*, by Jacques Duquesne (Grasset, 1965):

> "We are sure of God, but have no clear notion of what we are ourselves, or of where we are. . . ." This country parish priest expresses clearly enough what today's priests feel confusedly both at the sociological level and at the pastoral level. They are not clear on "what they are." And, in the first place, they do not have "a recognized social function," for the reason that they are no longer "situated" in today's social world.

One could quote a great many more such passages from recent writings on priests and religious. In France alone there was a new book every month on the priesthood in 1965, and the number has been added to steadily ever since. "Never before was so much written on the priest," says *Informations Catholiques Internationales* (May 1, 1966).

THE URGENCY OF THE PROBLEM

My purpose in quoting from these different reviews is to draw attention to a factor in the situation which is of great importance: the urgency of the over-all problem. That the affair is urgent becomes even more obvious when one reflects that the headlines and the magazine articles show only the tip of the iceberg. How big is the iceberg underneath? For every one priest or religious who makes a defiant statement or takes up a defiant stance, or who disobeys, how many priests and religious are there who experience, in varying degrees of intensity—or who deliberately suppress —a similar conflict within themselves? For every one priest or religious who has married, legally or illegally, how many are there in whose lives celibacy is not beneficial but, in varying degrees, an obstacle in their human, Christian development and to the full exercise of their ministry?

I would mention in passing however that, while rebellion and rebellious talk, and strong adverse criticism are not necessarily to be encouraged, there is this to be said for them: they are a sign of life. A great English Dominican, Father Vincent McNabb, used to say: "Lines of life, lines of danger." The only place where one can be guaranteed a complete and perpetual absence of tension and dissension is a cemetery. The defections from the religious and clerical life, however, are not of themselves a sign of life. They are tragic occurrences. They can, however, be turned to good account if they impart a sense of urgency to our awareness of the need for reform. It would be adding tragedy to tragedy if the defections merely led to a tightening of rules and regulations. This would lead to further defections, for it would be against the spirit of the Council (see *Decree on Religious Life,* par. 4).

The passages from the magazines do more than underline the urgency of the matter, however. Between them they also touch on many of the most important elements of the situation in which the priest and religious finds himself in the post-conciliar age. An element that seems to me to be of particular importance is the awareness which they manifest of priests (and religious), not as so many units living lives of their own, lives apart, but as human beings involved in, and affected by, people and institutions outside themselves. Thus, to take the last quotation first, the priest is no longer sure of what he is, because he is no longer situated "in today's social world." This implies that the priest's role is affected by his relationships with the world in which he lives. Then again the priest and religious are seen as being related to, and affected by, those in authority and the institutions and structure of the Church.

I suggest that it is of some importance to have an awareness of the priest and the religious as people who are involved in, and influenced by, a network of relationships: to the world, the Church, the authorities in the Church, the laity in the Church, the institutions of the Church. The Vatican Council has had a good deal to say on the priest and religious and on their relationships with these people and institutions. But it is important to remember that the lives and roles of priests and religious after Vatican II will also be affected—are being affected—by what the Council has had to say about these institutions and people themselves.

This is a matter of being aware that, when things around one change, this may effect a change in oneself. Thus, to take an imaginary analogy: if one were living on an island, a Gulliver ten feet high amongst a million Lilliputians six inches high; and if, overnight, the islanders all grew to ten feet tall, one's role among them would change considerably as a result of this change in them. (Similarly, one's relationship to the laity must needs be affected by the fact that the Vatican Council has increased their stature.) To take another analogy: if one's country is at war with another country, one may develop considerable animosity towards the enemy country. However, if one's country makes peace with the other country and, further, inaugurates a new policy of friendship towards its former enemy, this will demand a similar readjustment of attitude on one's own part, if one is to remain a loyal, patriotic citizen of one's country.

## THE CHURCH AND THE WORLD

This latter analogy brings us to the first major factor affecting clerical and religious life from outside, as it were. The attitude of the Church to the world, and the attitude of the world to the Church have profound repercussions on the role of the priest and the religious, and on their conception of their role.

I had better make clear in which sense I am using the word "world." I am using the word in the way that the *Constitution on the Church in the Modern World* uses it; a word, that is to say, which *in itself* has no theological connotations. Catholic theology uses the word "world" to convey much the same notion as is conveyed by the phrase, "God's creation" (Karl Rahner, *Concise Theological Dictionary*, World). But there is also another sense in which Christian theology, and especially Christian ascetical writing, uses the word "world" to denote something evil and to be avoided:

> The world (what Scripture calls "this" world, "this" aeon) means all those principalities and powers that are hostile to God, the tangible embodiment of sin in the world and everything in the world that incites to further sin. It is in this sense that the Christian is not to be "of the world," though he cannot help being "in" it (Jn. 17:11) (*ibid.*).

As is well known, there has always existed among Christians the temptation to exaggerate this tendency, to push it to extremes, thus forgetting the following:

> Even this sinful world is an object of God's love, needs redemption yet is redeemable, is already embraced by God's grace despite and in its sin, and its history will come to an end in *basileia*. Hence the Christian must come to grips with

it, notwithstanding its opposition to God, must uphold such true order as remains in the world in the strength of divine grace, must encourage the capacities within the world for sound development, carefully distinguishing these from its baser solicitations. . . . Thus Christianity knows no radical, irreconcilable dualism between God and the world; and Christian practice should not be guided by any such perverse idea (*ibid.*).

I use the word "world" in a sense which is neither a synonym for good nor a synonym for evil; this is the sense in which we use it in current secular speech, and it is the sense which it has in the title of the *Constitution on the Church in the Modern World,* and in its Preface:

The world the Council has in mind, then, is the world of men, the entire human family, its whole environment; the world which is the theater of human history, marked with man's industry, his triumphs and disasters. It is the world which the faithful believe to be made and sustained by the Creator's love. It was enslaved indeed to sin, but Christ crucified and risen from the dead has freed it, so that according to God's design it may be transformed and achieve its fulfillment.

The Church has changed its attitude to the world thus described, and this must profoundly affect the priest and the religious. In the article from *Études* quoted above, Henri Holstein suggested that the problems of today's priests and religious may in part be bound up with their attitude to the world in which we live. It may be that many of us are still living, camel-like, off a hump of ideas and attitudes about the world which are no longer relevant. He outlines three successive attitudes of the Church to its vocation to preach the salvation of Christ to the world: 1) From the beginning and during patristic times the Church conceived its role as being merely that of announcing Christ's salvation to the world. 2) Subsequently the Church saw its role as that of organizing the city of God on earth, of organizing and maintaining the kingdom of God on earth, Christendom. 3) Later, after the Renaissance, the Church defended the message of salvation which had been confided to it, against all assaults upon it.

The majority of today's priests and brothers have been brought up on that last attitude. We regarded those outside the Church as people from whom to expect hostility or as people with whom fraternization was impossible or undesirable. Consequently we tended to be on the defensive about ourselves and protective about the faith and the sacraments which had been committed to our care. Of course, we did not all realize that this was our attitude until we had caught glimpses of another possible attitude, or until we had read or heard the attitude described in bold, bald terms as "ghetto-mentality," "siege-mentality," "fortress-mentality," "closed-minds." We saw these words cropping up again and again in reports on the Ecumenical Council. We realized that they were often grossly misused and their meaning and extension exaggerated in that type of writing which can be classified as "conciliar folklore." We realized, for example, that one could scarcely classify the involvement of American Catholics in politics as being the expression of a "ghetto-mentality"; that there were many areas of Catholic activity and many Catholics of whom the descriptions were becoming progressively less true.

However, even after allowances had been made for exaggerations, and even after we had excluded everything and everybody to whom the description did not fully apply, we were still left with the uncomfortable conclusion that the cap fitted.

The change of attitude to which we are committed after the Council is considerable. It may be helpful if we try to see it in concrete terms, as follows: For the Christian three attitudes to the world are possible—understanding "the world" in the sense in which we use it in current speech, the sense in which it is not a synonym for evil, but for that compound of good and evil which is the world. The first of the three attitudes which the Christian can have towards the world is the one we have been describing, an attitude in which hostility plays a dominant part. This attitude leads the Christian to cut himself off from the world, more or less completely (the implication being that the more authentically Christian he wants to be, the more complete must be his alienation from the world), dismissing its values as being inimical to the Christian life. This attitude, it seems to me, is to be seen in the attitudes of many Catholics to the modern novel, to modern art (especially in churches), and to the modern theater.

The second attitude to the world is one which is possible but not lawful for the Christian. This is an attitude of friendship, but an attitude which leads to adopting the world's values (all of them, the bad as well as the good) and leaving Christ and one's Christian values behind. Thus not only will one fail to manifest Christ to the world, but one will jettison Christ, giving up one's Christian beliefs. One disadvantage of the dominance which the fortress-mentality had hitherto was that it bred a tendency to see this second approach as the only possible alternative to hostility to the world. In fact, there are many Catholics to this day who see loss of faith as the inevitable consequence —or, at the very least, the occupational hazard—of commerce with the world. In fact, one wonders if there is not a further disadvantage in the survival of the fortress-mentality into modern times: that not only has it kept certain Catholics outside the main stream of modern culture, it has also entailed that, when Catholics did become involved in the main stream of modern culture, they lost the faith in the process, because (in part, at any rate) they knew of no alternative to hostility save total surrender. Perhaps it is not accurate to say that they knew of no other alternative to hostility save total surrender; rather that they lacked the intellectual equipment for any other kind of commerce with the modern world.

There is, of course, another kind of commerce with the modern world. It is the third possibility open to the Christian, the kind of commerce with the modern world of which Pope John was the most dramatic exponent and example. Pope John approached the modern world in a spirit of friendship and concern, but also as the bearer of Christ to the world. And Pope John's own spirit is re-echoed in the *Constitution on the Church in the Modern World*: "For the Christian community is made up of men; . . . and they have received a message of salvation as something to be offered to everybody" (par. 1).

It may help towards an understanding of the change in attitude if we discuss some of the characteristics of the attitude of the Church to the modern world, as it can be gleaned from the conciliar documents and from the example and life of Pope John.

1) The change of attitude to the world is no mere gimmick: it is the logical outcome of the Church's taking stock of her own nature in the second half of the twentieth century:

> . . . the Second Vatican Council, having already examined more deeply the mystery of the Church, now speaks unhesitatingly not only to the Church's sons and to those who call on the name of Christ, but to all men, anxious to explain to all how it understands the presence and function of the Church in the world of today (*Church in the Modern World*, par. 2).

(How exactly the change of attitude is the logical outcome of what the Council has to say about the nature of the Church will become clearer as we outline some of the remaining characteristics of the new attitude.)

2) The keynote of the Church's attitude to the world is love and service, or loving service. Thus the concluding section of the *Constitution on the Church in the Modern World* (par. 91) urges all men to collaborate with the Church and with each other "under the impulse of love," and in the Preface the Constitution acknowledges that the Church "loves and respects" the human family. Father Edward Schillebeeckx, O.P., wrote recently:

> A future historian pouring over the dossiers of the Second Vatican Council may wonder what the Church actually did in that different twentieth century with its wars, its misery and chaos; a century also of *aggiornamento* of the entire social-economic and political life; a critical moment in the history of the world. In the words of Pope Paul VI, in his address at the opening of the fourth session, he will find that "the Church loved." In this Council, said the Pope, alluding to the gospel story that tells how Jesus looked upon a youth and loved him (Mk. 10:21), the Church has looked upon the world and fallen in love with it. "This council is a solemn act of love towards humanity; . . . here on earth the Church is not an end in herself, she is here to serve all."

Father Schillebeeckx comments: "As a loving community the Church is everyone's servant" (*Balance Sheet of the Council*, DO.C, dossier n. 66-1). This theme runs through many of the Council's documents. The Preface to the *Constitution on the Church in the Modern World* ends with the following words: "The Church is moved by no earthly ambition; she wants one thing only: led by the Holy Spirit to carry on the work of Christ, who came into this world to witness to the truth—to save, not to judge, to serve, not to be served." The same theme is enunciated in the *Consti-*

*tution on the Church*: ". . . although the Church needs human resources to carry out her mission, she is not set up to seek earthly glory, but to proclaim humility and self-sacrifice, even by her own example" (par. 8).

It hardly needs to be said that if these words apply to the Church as a whole they are especially applicable to priests and religious. The following quotations make the point explicitly: "Priests are the servants of all . . ." (*Decree on the Priesthood*, par. 6). "Priests . . . must join their labors to those of the laity following the example of the Master who came among men 'not to be served but to serve others and to give his life a ransom for many' (Mt. 20:28)" (*Decree on the Priesthood*, par. 9). "Seminarians should understand very plainly that they are called not to domination or to honors, but to give themselves over entirely to God's service and the pastoral ministry" (*Decree on Seminaries*, par. 9).

It will be noted that there is nothing very new in all this. This is no new doctrine; it has always been Christian teaching. What is relevant for us in the second half of the twentieth century is the authoritative and urgent insistence that we put it into practice. If every priest and religious were able to project this image of the Church as Pope John did, that would be something of untold consequence in the history of the Church. As Father Schillebeeckx reflected in a slightly different context, some of these phrases—"self-sacrifice," "humility," "to serve, not to be served," "the servants of all"—sound somewhat hollow when we begin to apply them to ourselves. Father Schillebeeckx remarked that the "outcome of this Council is not a result, but a mandate" (*loc. cit.*).

3) Not merely is the Church, its ministers and religious especially, committed to living service, it is also itself a sign and an instrument of unity: "By her relationship with Christ,

the Church is a kind of sacrament or sign of intimate union with God, and of the unity of all mankind. She is also an instrument for the achievement of such union and unity" (*Constitution on the Church*, par. 1). "[The Council] offers to mankind the honest assistance of the Church in fostering that brotherhood of all men which corresponds to this destiny of theirs" (*Church in the Modern World*, par. 3). This has been translated into practical terms in the priest's life by the *Decree on the Priesthood*:

> The purpose of the priesthood in the midst of the laity is to achieve unity of love. This is what St. Paul had in mind when he wrote: "Love one another with brotherly affection trying to be first in showing courtesy" (Rom. 12:10). Priests must try to weld the divine elements of their flock into a whole community so that none of the faithful will feel excluded. . . . If they are good shepherds priests will realize their personal obligation to bring back those who have ceased to receive the sacraments or even to practice the faith.
>
> Those Christians who belong to churches not fully in communion with us must not be forgotten. Of this fact the decree on Ecumenism reminds us. Nor can we exclude from our concern those who do not acknowledge Christ as their Savior (par. 9).

4) The Church is pledged to share the world's joys, hope, fears, and sufferings. Thus we Christians are committed not merely to awareness of the problems and hopes of our fellow-men—be they Northern Irish, Protestants, or Viet Cong—but to share them:

> The joy and hope, the sorrow and anxiety of the men of our time, especially of the poor and of those who are in any way suffering; these Christ's disciples make their own, and there is nothing human that does not find an echo in their hearts (*Church in the Modern World*, par. 1).

This degree of involvement with other men and women—whatever their race or beliefs—obviously ought not to go hand-in-hand with an abandonment of Christian beliefs and standards. For priests, especially, it must go hand-in-hand with a certain "set-apartness." The *Decree on the Priesthood* puts the matter supremely well:

> Priests are taken from among men and appointed for men in the things which pertain to God, in order to offer gifts and sacrifices for sins. Hence they deal with other men as with brothers. This was the way that the Lord Jesus, the Son of God, a man sent by the Father to men, dwelt among us and willed to become like his brothers in all things except sin. The holy Apostles imitated him, and blessed Paul, the teacher of the Gentiles, who was set apart for the gospel of God (Rom. 1:1), declares that he became all things to all men that he might save all.
>
> By their vocation and ordination, priests of the New Testament are indeed set apart in a certain sense within the midst of God's people. But this is so, not that they may be separated from this people or from any men, but that they may be totally dedicated to the work for which the Lord has raised them up. They cannot be ministers of Christ unless they are witnesses and dispensers of a life other than this earthly one. But they cannot be of service to men if they remain strangers to the life and conditions of men (par. 3).

In the nature of things, it was not to be expected that the *Decree on the Renewal of Religious Life* would be quite as specific about the involvement of religious with the world. The reason for this is that the Decree had to be applicable both to secular institutes and to Carthusian monks—obviously the degree of involvement with the world will vary from one type of institute to another. However, the Decree does state that:

> Communities should promote among their members suitable awareness of contemporary human conditions and of the needs of the Church. For if their members can combine the burning zeal of an apostle with wise judgments, made in the light of faith, concerning the circumstances of the modern world, they will be able to come to the aid of men more effectively (par. 2 d).

Later the decree asserts that the "life hidden with Christ," which religious lead, "is the source and stimulus of love of one's neighbor for the world's salvation and the building up of the Church. The practice of the evangelical counsels themselves is quickened and ruled by this same love" (par. 6).

5) A theme which was given increasing prominence as the Council progressed was that of poverty, both the practice of poverty within the Church, and the obligation on the Church to be specially involved with the poor and afflicted all over the world. It was mentioned in *The Message to Humanity*, and if the Church of the twentieth century will become once more involved with the poor and the down-trodden as Christ was, this will in no small measure prove to have been due to the charismatic example of Pope John. The theme of the Church's involvement with the poor recurs through several of the documents:

> Christ was sent by the Father "to bring good news to the poor, to heal the contrite of heart" (Lk. 4:18), "to seek and to save what was lost" (Lk. 19:10). Similarly, the Church encompasses with love all those who are suffering and afflicted with human weakness. Indeed, she recognizes in the poor and suffering the likeness of her poor and suffering Founder. She does all she can to relieve their need and in them she strives to serve Christ (*The Constitution on the Church*, par. 8).

# 2: *Part of God's People*

The opening paragraph of the *Constitution on the Church in the Modern World* makes the point that the members of the Church form a brotherhood with all the people of the world and that the Church shares—or is committed to sharing—the joys and sorrows of men, of all men. Having made the point, the Constitution then goes on to give the reason for such involvement of the Church with the world:

> For the Christian community is made up of men; they are brought together in Christ, guided by the Holy Spirit along their pilgrim way to the Father's kingdom, and they have received a message of salvation as something to be offered to everybody. Hence the Christian community feels itself closely linked with the human race and its history (par. 1).

It is by now commonplace to remark that, in passages such as this, the Council is regarding the Church, not primarily as a hierarchically structured institution, but as a community, God's people. However, one suspects that we have not yet begun to understand, and to *feel in our bones,* what this means. It is primarily a shifting of emphasis: the Church, in talking about its own nature, sees itself first and foremost as a community, and secondly as a *hierarchically structured* community. That is not to say that this changed way of looking at the Church excludes the hierarchy, for God's people is composed of the hierarchy, the clergy and religious, as well as the laity.

A JURIDICAL CONCEPT OF THE CHURCH
One of the difficulties in appreciating how great a change is involved here is that we are in the realm of broad

generalities. As yet there is little in the way of specific concrete change or directives to show. But there would seem to be no doubt that this way of thinking about the Church will have profound repercussions on clerical and religious life. One can, however, have some inkling as to how great the change will be if one recalls that the kind of thinking about the Church to which all of us were accustomed from our youth was one in which "the Church" was synonymous with the clergy and the hierarchy. I am speaking now about attitudes deriving from a specific theological position. In the past our theology of the Church had been dominated by a juridical concept of the Church. If one thinks of the Church in exclusively juridical terms, one will *tend* to think of it in terms of two groups or classes of people, and—further— one will tend to think of each group in terms of its own function. One of the classes is composed of people who make and administer laws, and the other of the subjects who obey them. One will tend to forget in practice that subjects have any other function than to obey.

Undoubtedly, this way of looking at things was becoming more and more anachronistic, especially after the growth and development of Catholic action, and after the teaching of Pope Pius XI and Pope Pius XII on the role of the laity. One had a situation in which the laity were in fact doing far more than *obeying*, and—apart from the work of pioneers like Congar and Philips—much current theology and current attitudes among the clergy and laity had not yet fully caught up with this fact. The situation has vastly improved since the Council, but the old attitudes linger on. One can still frequently detect an instructive difference between what people say about the Church when the context invites them to advert to its nature, and what they say about the Church in other contexts. Thus, if an average Catholic, layman or priest, is asked what the Church is, and who constitute its members, his reply will probably manifest an advertence to the place and role of the laity (and lesser clergy) in the Church. However, such advertence is often lacking in other contexts, particularly if there is question of the Church *doing something*.

One has in mind here unreflected, spontaneous statements about the Church which sometimes reveal those attitudes which lie partly above and partly below the level of consciousness and which frequently have more effect on one's actions and decisions than one realizes. This, it seems to me, has considerable relevance in the present situation. Having been brought up, most of us, on the more juridical concept of the Church, we were *more* conscious of the lines of authority, from pope to bishops to priests to laity, and *less* conscious of the family ties, the links of a shared life, of charity. And let us reflect, too, that we did not merely *learn* the juridical concept of the Church in our theology classes, we also *absorbed* it from our parents, in our parishes, in our Sunday or daily worship. This is why I suggest it still survives, like last winter's snows, in the nooks and crannies of our spirits. It will not have been fully eradicated by reading the Council documents, nor by a few years' exposure to a more community-based worship. Thus a perceptive English theologian, Cornelius Ernst, O.P., could say even of Charles Davis after he had renounced his allegiance to the Church that his thinking about the Church was, unconsciously, pre-conciliar. He said that, in describing a clash between personal values and the institutions of the Church, the only institution present to Davis' mind and emotions was authority, which is but part of the structure of the Church. The sacraments are also an institution, and so—even—is the community.[1]

It might be a useful exercise in this post-conciliar age to devise tests to enable us to ascertain how deeply the Council's thinking on the Church has penetrated our attitudes and the wellsprings of our actions. Father Yves Congar, O.P., has remarked that, as the bishops assembled for the opening of the Council in 1962, if one had asked them whence they received their episcopal powers, ninety-eight per cent of them would have replied: "From the pope, by canonical institution." A year later, he went on, ninety-eight per cent of them gave the following reply to the same question:

> We hold our powers, in the first place, and basically, in virtue of our episcopal consecration, which is sacramental. In virtue of this consecration, one is in the communion with the head of the college of bishops and with its members, one is constituted a member of the body of the bishops and invested with the triple function of sanctifying, teaching, and governing.[2]

## THE REAL CONCEPT OF THE CHURCH

A question like the following may help one to test one's *real* (as opposed to notional) understanding of the nature of the Church: When one is referring in fact only to those who are invested with authority in the Church, does one spontaneously use the word "the Church" to describe them —as in a question such as, "Why is the Church so slow about solving the birth-control problem?" Another attitude may sometimes complement the attitude revealed by such a question: it is the attitude which fails fully to realize the implications of one's membership of the Church, fails to be aware that when a responsibility falls on the Church as a

[1]See *The Tablet* (London, January 6, 1967).
[2]*Informations Catholiques Internationales* (January 1, 1966).

whole, it falls on oneself too, as a member of the Church. Thus many a person who asks questions such as: "Why doesn't the Church speak out more strongly against racial injustice?" might be quite surprised to be told: "You are the Church, what are you doing about it?" In 1946 Pope Pius XII occasioned a good deal of surprise when he said of the laity: "They are the Church."[3] Writing eight years later, Monsignor Gerard Philips of Louvain, Belgium, could write: "Even many Catholics are surprised at this statement."[4]

So much has happened since Monsignor Philips wrote these words, that by now he might have difficulty in discovering a Catholic of whom his remark holds true. The statement of Pius XII does not occasion surprise any more. But it is one thing for the laity to know and accept what the Pope meant. It is another to absorb it, so that it sinks into the marrow of their bones.

It is more germane to our present purpose, however, to remark that it may be still more difficult for religious and clergy, especially the senior clergy, to make the transition from notional acceptance to real acceptance of the Pope's statement. The future development of Catholicism may depend, to a greater degree than many of us realize, on the ability of priests and religious to adjust to the shift in emphasis from hierarchy to community, to adjust to the irruption of the layman into what used to be thought of as a tight little "ecclesiastical" (as opposed to *ecclesial*) Church. (One apologizes for the tautology, but hopes that it is justifiable.) But it is not only a question of the clergy seeing the laity as part of the Church; clergy and religious must learn to see *themselves* as members of a people, a com-

[3] Address to the College of Cardinals, February 20, 1946.
[4] *The Role of the Laity in the Church* (Cork), p. 5.

munity. They must learn to shuffle off the centuries-old habit of expecting all decisions and all initiatives from higher up. They must understand their own place and role in the community, and not merely their relations with an awakened laity. Again I would emphasize that, what is in question is an understanding which seeps into every nook and cranny of one's mind and imagination, and which has won one's wholehearted acceptance at the emotional level.

It is instructive to recall a letter written by Cardinal John Henry Newman about the danger of keeping the laity at arms-length in matters of Christian concern. In a letter to a Mr. Fotrell he recalled his abortive attempt to set up a Catholic university in Dublin, Ireland. In the course of the letter he wrote:

> One of the chief evils which I deplored in the management of the affairs of the university twenty years ago when I was in Ireland was the absolute refusal, with which my urgent representations were met, that the Catholic laity should be allowed to cooperate with the archbishops in the work.
>
> So far as I can see, there are ecclesiastics all over Europe whose policy it is to keep the laity at arms-length, and hence the laity have been disgusted and become infidel, and only two parties exist, both ultras in opposite directions. I came away from Ireland with the distressing fear that in that Catholic country, in like manner, there was to be an antagonism as time went on between the hierarchy and the educated classes.
>
> You will be doing the greatest possible benefit to the Catholic cause all over the world, if you succeed in making the university a middle station at which laity and clergy can meet, *so as to learn to understand and yield to each other,* and from which, as from a common ground, they may act in union upon an age which is running headlong into infidelity.[5]

There is a story, also related by Mr. Ward, of a cleric of Cardinal Newman's time who manifested just the an-

[5]In Wilfrid Ward, *The Life of John Henry Cardinal Newman,* II, pp. 397-98. Italics mine.

tagonism to the laity of which the Cardinal wrote. An anonymous attack on Newman had been published in the *Weekly Register* and a group of Catholic laymen had written and signed a letter of protest against the attack. This incensed a Monsignor Talbot, a man who had little patience with this example of what he deemed lay meddling in Church affairs. "What is the province of the laity?" he wrote in a letter to Cardinal Manning, "To hunt, to shoot, to entertain. These matters they understand, but to meddle with ecclesiastical matters they have no right at all, and this affair of Newman is a matter purely ecclesiastical."[6]

It is easy to convince oneself that Monsignor Talbot's attitude is wholly remote from present realities. It is true, of course, that no present-day cleric would discuss the problem of the layman's role *solely* in terms of the upper classes, as Monsignor Talbot did. It is as though, in Monsignor Talbot's eyes, in this context only the upper classes deserved even the scant consideration that he gave them. As for the middle and lower classes, one did not even consider them in such a context. However, it is one thing to have left such class consciousness behind. It is quite another to have developed an attitude to membership in the Church that is fully in keeping with Vatican II.

It is a matter of record that the first and second drafts of the *Constitution on the Church* presented to the Council fathers in 1962 and 1963 respectively, still manifested a juridical conception of the Church in the very arrangement of the chapters. In both these drafts, the chapter on the hierarchy came before the section on God's people—thereby implying, someone facetiously remarked, that the hierarchy did not belong to God's people! In the third draft, and in

[6]*Ibid.*, p. 147.

the fourth and final draft, the order was changed. In the new arrangement, the section on God's people became chapter two, and the chapter on the hierarchy became chapter three.

More is involved here then mere arithmetic or convenience of arrangement. As Father Colman O'Neill, O.P., says, by this rearrangement "a new perspective is given to the whole constitution."[7] Father Edward Schillebeeckx, O.P., comments: "The stresses have been heavily transposed: the hierarchy itself has relinquished its religious monopoly within the Church and has attributed this religiousness in the first instance to God's people, of which it is the guardian and servant."[8]

THE CHURCH AS COMMUNITY

One does not, of course, wish to convey the impression that the Council's entire teaching on the Church as community is to be deduced from a change in the order of chapters of the *Constitution on the Church.* The new emphasis pervades the entire *Constitution:* the change of order was merely a dramatic indication that, at a certain point, the new emphasis had gained the acceptance of the majority.

A number of consequences follow from the new emphasis, consequences which will notably affect the way in which the priest and the religious conceive their role in the community and their relationship with the other members of it.

One is tempted to say that as priests, religious, and laity become more accustomed to seeing the Church as a community, primarily, rather than as a juridical structure, they

7In Austin Flannery, O.P., Ed., *Vatican II: The Church Constitution* (Chicago: The Priory Press, 1966), p. 15.
8*Balance Sheet of the Council,* DO.C., dossier n. 66-1.

will in consequence become more conscious of what they share—their common baptism—than of what differentiates between them. It might be more realistic, however, to acknowledge that this may not necessarily happen and to fall back on the assertion that awareness of the Church as a community is, in the logic of the case, conducive to a more lively awareness of common bonds.

Here, one is not thinking solely in terms of relations between clergy and laity, or between subjects and those in authority. One is thinking also of the bonds among the laity themselves, or among priests and religious themselves. If one thinks of the Church almost exclusively in terms of juridical structures, not only does this *tend* to make one less aware of the bonds between oneself and those in authority, there is this further disadvantage, that it does little to help one realize that there are bonds between one and the believers at one's own level. One tends to think of one's Christian life as a kind of solo flight towards God, a flight that is assisted by the various strata of authority above one.

The outlook I have been describing is familiar enough to most of us. We have been brought up, more or less, on this. But this way of looking at one's own involvement in the Church has been swept away by Vatican II:

> At all times and in every race, anyone who fears God and does what is right has been acceptable to him (*cf.* Acts 10:35). He has, however, willed to make men holy and to save them, not as individuals without any bond or link between them, but rather to make them into a people who might acknowledge him and serve him in holiness (*Constitution on the Church*, par. 9).

The temptation for the Christian to see himself as a solo operator, or, rather, as the individual recipient of God's love, was most manifest for some people at the time of

Holy Communion. I recall administering Holy Communion in an excellent girl's school. As each girl whispered a barely audible "Amen," in response to my clear, "The Body of Christ," it was borne in on me that the good nuns had taught the girls to say the word thus inaudibly. They felt, no doubt, that no other human being should intrude on a moment of such intimate communion with God. And yet such individualism could not be more incongruous than at the moment of reception of the sacrament whose effect is the unification of the Body of Christ. Far from seeing Holy Communion as a meeting with Christ so private that it turns one's brothers in Christ into intruders, one should see it for what it is: a communion with Christ and with all other men, especially those who are nearest to one, nearest by ties of blood or Christian fellowship.

It must not be imagined that when one sees the Church primarily as a community one eliminates all differences and distinctions, as though one had reduced the whole Church to a flat, level surface. It is not here that the difference lies between the juridical approach and the more theological approach. The problem with the juridical approach is that it tends to describe in negative terms, merely, those who lack jurisdiction. (Nor is this just a cumbersome way of saying that the canonist does not see them at all. He sees them all right, but only as the have-nots, an ecclesiastical proletariat.) In itself, and when complemented by a theological appraisal, this description is justifiable; its inadequacies become manifest, however, when it is put forward as the total, or near-total, view of the Church. For this *tends* to be a view of the Church as a structure of which the laity form no part. In his *Lay People in the Church*, Father Yves Congar, O.P., says that in the canonical view of the Church, lay people "are negative creatures" (p. 15).

The theological view of the Church, however, enables us to see the Church as a structure in which layman, monk, and cleric all have a place. Not that the canonist would ever consciously see the layman as being outside the Church. But his tendency is to see him as not fully belonging to the Church. (The obverse of this—in a related context—is the tendency to see the superior of a community as not fully part of the community. Thus, we speak of "Father Superior and community," instead of either, "The community," or "Father Superior and the other members of the community." And at the Council some bishops preferred to speak of Our Lady *and* the Church, instead of Our Lady *in* the Church.)

The fuller, more theological, view of the Church outlined in chapter two of the *Constitution on the Church* sees the Church, first of all, as the community of the baptized:

> Christ the Lord, High Priest taken from among men (Heb. 5:1-5), made the new people "a kingdom of priests to God, his Father" (Ap. 1:6; *cf.* 5:9-10). The baptized, by regeneration and the anointing of the Holy Spirit, are consecrated to be a spiritual house and a holy priesthood that through all the works of Christian men they may offer spiritual sacrifices and proclaim the perfections of him who had called them out of darkness into his marvellous light (*cf.* 1 Pt. 2:4-10) (par. 10).

If priests and religious realize and feel in their bones the fundamental and all-pervasive importance of baptism in the structure of the Christian Church, they will at once acquire a deeper appreciation both of the ecclesial context and dimension of their own vocations and of the priestly character and the holiness of their brothers and sisters in Christ who are neither priests nor religious. Thus:

> Though they differ essentially and not only in degree, the common priesthood of the faithful and the ministerial or hier-

archical priesthood are nonetheless ordered one to another; each in its own proper way shares in the one priesthood of Christ. The ministerial priest, by the sacred power he has, forms and rules the priestly people; in the person of Christ he effects the Eucharistic sacrifice and offers it to God in the name of all the people (*Constitution on the Church*, par. 10).

The *Decree on the Ministry and Life of Priests* speaks about the "royal priesthood" of the faithful in its opening chapter, and then goes on to say that "the Lord has established certain ministers among the faithful in order to join them together in one body" (par. 2). There is a moral to be drawn from the ecclesial origin and the ecclesial purpose of the priest's vocation, and it is drawn in paragraph three: "Priests are taken from among men and appointed for men in the things which pertain to God, in order to offer gifts and sacrifices for sins. *Hence they deal with other men as brothers.*" (Italics mine.)

BROTHERHOOD AND INVOLVEMENT

This sense of brotherhood ought to be especially marked in the priests' relations with their bishops, their fellow priests and religious: "Hence it is very important that all priests, whether diocesan or religious, always help one another to be fellow workers on behalf of truth. Each one therefore is united by special bonds of apostolic charity, ministry, and brotherhood, with the other members of his presbytery" (par. 8).

The religious, too, is reminded that his vocation is ecclesial in origin and purpose. In the *Constitution on the Church* we read: "Being means to and instruments of love, the evangelical counsels unite those who practice them to the Church and her mystery in a special way. It follows that the spiritual life of such Christians should be dedicated to the welfare of the entire Church" (par. 44).

The same point is made in the *Decree on the Renewal of the Religious Life*: "All institutes should share in the life of the Church. They should make their own and should foster to the best of their ability, in a manner consonant with their own natures, her initiatives and plans in biblical, liturgical, dogmatic, pastoral, ecumenical, and social matters" (par. 2 d).

About a year before the promulgation of the *Decree on the Renewal of Religious Life*, Pope Paul VI spoke of this matter to a large audience of nuns at Castelgondolfo. He made it clear that, in his view, it was not at all superfluous to admonish religious to develop a sense of involvement in the Church:

> It sometimes happens that certain religious families are lacking in awareness of the Church, or do not sufficiently cultivate it. They live apart, finding that all their interests are satisfied within their own communities, and they know little of what happens outside their own work, to which they are wholly dedicated. . . . Such isolation is not an ideal position for the religious; it robs her of the great and complete vision of God's divine design for our salvation and for our sanctification. It is not a privilege to remain on the outskirts of the life of the Church, constructing for oneself a spirituality which is cut off from the circulation of word, of grace and charity in the Catholic community of brothers in Christ.[9]

It is not surprising that the clergy's relinquishment of "its religious monopoly" (and the laity's consequent "promotion") should be most palpably experienced (and at the same time fostered) in the reformed liturgical celebrations. The liturgical *aggiornamento* had a long start on most other sorts of *aggiornamento* in the Church, as was evidenced by the fact that, of all the documents to go before the

[9]Address of September 8, 1964; translation in *Supplement to Doctrine and Life* (n. 11), pp. 146-47.

Council, the *Constitution on the Sacred Liturgy* suffered least change through conciliar amendments. The document offered to the Council by the preparatory committee met the requirements—almost in their entirety—of the pastoral and reforming Council.

But there is more to it than that. The liturgy is "the summit toward which the activity of the Church is directed," as the *Constitution on the Liturgy* tells us (par. 10). Further, the Christian people in its entirety, lay, religious, and cleric, is a priestly people and a religious, or holy, people. The *Constitution on the Liturgy* quotes the proud phrases of St. Peter—"a chosen race, a royal priesthood, a holy nation, a redeemed people"—in the article which gives the *raison d'être* of the laity's participation in the liturgy: it is something to which they have "a right and an obligation by reason of their baptism" (par. 14).

We have entered on a changing pattern of relationships between the different categories of the "royal priesthood." One can sense something of the progress of the change in the hesitations one experiences with regard to the use of the words "priest" and "religious." One experiences an increasing reluctance to use the words in the limited application they have had hitherto. One feels the need to employ such terms as "baptismal priesthood" and "pastoral priesthood."[10] What is happening is that we are slowly developing an awareness of the Church as a people, a family, in which the relationships of *love* and *brotherhood* are gradually assuming greater importance than those of *authority* and *subjection*. It is not that authority and subjection to authority are passing away, but that their meaning is being re-

[10]See Pierre A. Liègé, O.P., "Baptême et Sacerdoce," in a special issue of *Prêtres Diocesains* (February-March, 1966), 57-64.

interpreted—sometimes in the context of painful experience —in the light of love and brotherhood.

A remarkable passage in the fourth chapter of the *Constitution on the Church,* the chapter on the laity, offers much food for thought in this connection:

> As the laity through the divine choice have Christ as their brother, who, though Lord of all, came not to be served but to serve (*cf.* Mt. 20:28), they also have as brothers those in the sacred ministry who by teaching, by sanctifying, and by ruling with the authority of Christ so nourish the family of God that the new commandment of love may be fulfilled by all. As St. Augustine very beautifully put it: "When I am frightened by what I am to you, then I am consoled by what I am with you. To you I am the bishop, with you I am a Christian. The first is an office, the second a grace; the first a danger, the second salvation" (par. 32).

By way of a postscript, one adds as a commentary on the foregoing (though the roles of the two passages might also be reversed), the following hard-hitting paragraph from the English interdenominational fortnightly, *The New Christian.* The paragraph is taken from an editorial on the suspension of Father Herbert McCabe, the English Dominican, and his removal from the editorship of *New Blackfriars:*

> On the broader front, however, this particularly distressing incident raises the question of freedom in the Church and, with it, a key theological judgment about the nature of the Christian community. Of the latter it may be said with confidence that the New Testament and the mainstream of Christian tradition sees the Church as a community of love and freedom. Because the individuals who constitute the Church have surrendered their lives to Christ, the corporate life of the Christian community reflects something of the quality of life which belongs to the kingdom of God. This is not to say that the Church may gaily abandon all forms of discipline. The institutional aspect of its life demands the cohesion which comes through order and control. But the discipline of the Church must be nearer in spirit and application to that of the family than to

that of the prison service. The Christian fellowship is a company of mature persons and not an ecclesiastical remand home in which a group of delinquent adolescents is subjected to the will of those who are presumed to be of clearer vision.[11]

[11](February 23, 1967).

43

# 3: Changing for Tradition's Sake

> Tradition . . . implies . . . the will to learn from the experience of those who have studied and created before us; the aim of this lesson is to receive the vitality of their inspiration and to continue their creative work in its original spirit, which thus, in a new generation, is born again with the freedom, the youthfulness, and the promise which it originally possessed (Yves Congar, O.P., *Tradition in the Life of the Church*).

> A state without the means of change is without the means of its own conservation (Edmund Burke, *The French Revolution*).

> But there are people who are attracted by the durability of stone. They want to be massive and impenetrable, they do not want to change: where would change lead them? This is in origin a fear of oneself and fear of the truth (Jean Paul Sartre, *Reflections*).

For religious, more than for any other category in the Church, the Ecumenical Council is a case of "do it yourself." There is a sense in which this is true for every member of the Church, as Pope John was frequently at pains to emphasize. In his capital statement on the aims of the Ecumenical Council he said: "The principal aims will be to promote the growth of the Catholic faith and a renewal of morality amongst Christians. . . ."[1] The phrase "growth of the Catholic faith" did not refer to numerical or geographical growth, but to believers' growth in understanding of their faith. And

[1]Encyclical, *Ad Petri Cathedram*, July 3, 1959. This and all subsequent translations quoted here are *Doctrine and Life* translations.

"renewal of morality" must not be taken to mean merely the elimination of misconduct, but growth in holiness. Thus it was that Pope John could go on to speak of the completion of the Council's work as "a wonderful spectacle of truth, unity, and charity."

The ultimate criterion of the success of the Council, therefore, is the holiness of the Church's members. The sixteen Council documents will remain but so much paper and printer's ink until they have been understood and translated into attitudes and actions. Religious share with all other members of the Church the responsibility for putting the Council documents into practice.

But there is another kind of renewal than the personal renewal of which we have been speaking: it is renewal of the structures of the community which is the Church. Here again one can differentiate between renewal of the structures of the Church as a whole—for example, renewal of the liturgical rites, or of the Canon Law—and renewal of the structures of particular communities which exist within the Church. To this category belongs the renewal of religious orders, congregations, and secular institutes. The Council refrained from detailed structural renewal of religious communities, confining itself to general directives. The reason for this is that the primitive spirit of an institute must needs be normative in shaping such a program of renewal. Consequently the task were best confided to the members of each institute, for they can be presumed to have readiest access to its primitive spirit.

Thus each religious institute is being asked to accomplish in its own regard—and in the spirit of the Ecumenical Council—what the Council set out to accomplish for the whole Church. The Council's purpose was well described by Pope John, in words which, *mutatis mutandis,* might well be taken as a headline by religious in their present endeavors:

> The whole purpose of the coming Ecumenical Council is to restore its splendor to the face of the Church of Christ, as it was in her primitive simplicity and purity; to present it again as its Divine Founder fashioned it: without stain or wrinkle, *sine macula et ruga*. After her long journey down the ages, the Church is still far from her goal of transformation into triumphant eternity. That is why she must pause from time to time to take counsel, endeavoring, with loving care, to rediscover the outlines of her fervent youth.[2]

One might say, therefore, that the Ecumenical Council has imposed two kinds of task on religious. One of these they share with other members of the Church: it is to *implement* the Council's decrees, both those which refer to all members of the Church and those which refer to themselves, as religious and/or as priests. Over and above that kind of task, however, there is another, one analogous to the process of decision-making which the Council fathers themselves exercised for the whole Church. This is the renewal and adaptation of their own institutes within the letter and spirit of the Council.

ALL THE MEMBERS ARE RESPONSIBLE

Moreover, and this is a point of fundamental importance, both kinds of task are laid not merely on the superiors of an institute, but on all the members. The point is made explicitly, both in the *Decree on the Renewal of Religious Life* and in the *Norms*[3] for its implementation:

> Effective renewal and right adaptation cannot be achieved save with the cooperation of all the members of an institute (*Decree*, par. 4).

[2]Address on the occasion of the inauguration of the work of the preparatory commission, November 13, 1960.
[3]The *Norms for the Implementation of the Decree on Religious Life* (Dominican Publications, Dublin).

> It is the institutes themselves which have the main responsibility for renewal and adaptation. . . . The cooperation of all superiors and subjects is necessary for the renewal of their own religious lives, for the preparation of the spirit which should animate the chapter, for the accomplishment of their task . . . (*Norms*, par. 1).

Naturally, the responsibility for reform does not fall in the same way on superiors and on subjects. The decree states that "it is for the competent authorities, alone, and especially for general chapters, to establish the norms for up-to-date renewal and to legislate for it." This provision—one suspects—offers cold comfort to members of institutes whose superiors lack understanding of the spirit of the Council and manifest little willingness or ability to change. While one sympathizes with religious who find themselves in that position, one suggests that no other sort of provision could have been contemplated. Any person in authority can—because he is human—yield to the temptation to paternalistic or tyrannical behavior; but in the Church the remedy for such a situation must be sought in recourse to the law and the constituted channels of authority. Outside these lies the greater danger of the tyranny of anarchy. In any case, esteem for law and authority must remain constants of the Church no matter how the exercise of authority and its role may change in the present period of renewal. Esteem for the law and for authority must not be allowed to become a casualty of the period of transition.

However, the temptation of those in authority is to imagine that only the imprudence of subjects can diminish esteem for authority. Unfortunately, sometimes it is precisely the imprudence (using the word in St. Thomas' sense, in which it is far from being synonymous with caution) of superiors which invites evasion of the law or imprudent action contrary to the law. This is especially true at the present time. The knowledge that a changing pattern of authority is emerging in the Church is accessible to all and is likely to have a special impact on the young, who are more receptive to the idea of change and not many of whom are superiors. Further, it is obvious too that this is involved in a wider pattern of changes in the Church, and that these changes are demanded by the Council.

If subjects find that their superiors are unwilling to change their manner of exercising authority, or that they are unwilling, or even reluctant, to embark on the changes inspired by the Council, they will not always be able to reject the suspicion that their superiors are disobedient. The strain on subjects can become intolerable at times if insufficient docility to the higher authority of the Council on the part of superiors is linked with an insistence on absolute docility to themselves on the part of their own subjects. Subjects sometimes have the impression that they are being asked, in the name of obedience, to acquiesce in a passive resistance to the Council. Nor is such suspicion always dissipated if superiors, instead of remaining wholly immobile, embark on a program of change which appears excessively slow and cautious to many of their subjects. For a paternalistic superior can, unwittingly, objectivize and universalize his own reluctance to change and his disenchantment with *aggiornamento*. Thus he may make his own subjective reactions the norm for the rate of change. And his own attitudes may affect even the *quality* of the movement forward. There are (at least) two ways of moving forward. One is when the motive power is outside one and one's own sole contribution is to slow down the rate of motion. The other is when one is oneself the source of the impulsion forward. One might, in fact, then be moving forward at no higher speed than in the first example, but the quality of one's movement will be different. It will be voluntary movement and it will be obvious that one's heart is in it. Besides, one will watch where one is going and will select the best route; and one will prepare the way before one if that is needed.

NEED FOR RENEWAL NOW OFFICIAL

It may not be inappropriate to remark, at this stage, that it is now official teaching that religious orders and congregations are in need of renewal and adaptation. One suspects that it is just this that some religious are unwilling to accept. But, as Father Gregory Baum, O.S.A., has written: "It is no longer up to general chapters or individual superiors to decide whether their institutes are in need of renewal. The Council has decided this for all religious communities."[4] Of course, if one is very literal-minded, one may object that nowhere in the *Decree* or in the *Norms* is it stated that "all religious institutes are in need of renewal." But we must not allow the Council fathers' politeness to blind us to the patent implication of the *Decree*: the whole exercise would be pointless if there were no need for renewal. In fact, the *Norms* go further, asserting that renewal must be a *constant* preoccupation of religious; it "cannot be achieved once for all: it needs to be fostered continually . . ." (par. 19). In any case, it ought not to have needed an Ecumenical Council to convince us that we need to change. That it did need a council is due to the fact that we had all been habituated to a relative immobilism for several hundred years. Thus the greatest change of all has been that from a suspicious attitude towards the notion of change to an acceptance of change as a condition of life. Once we tended to see *change* and *tradition* as contraries,

[4]Commentary on the *Decree on the Renewal of Religious Life of Vatican II* (New York: Paulist Press), p. 30.

as enemies. We are now coming to see them as allies, to realize that change can be on the side of tradition (living tradition), that at times one must change *for the sake of tradition.* There comes a stage when, if a society does not change, does not adapt to changing times, it will sink into irrelevance and ineptitude. As Sister M. Cecilia Oddie, O.P., writes:

> Surely we can learn a great deal by applying the results of years of biological research in the natural course of evolution in the world of animals and plants, a world in which we take our place. Any society that hopes to survive must be able to adapt itself to changes in its environment, because it depends on this environment for its intake of new material and energy.[5]

However, it is not biology but theology which is our most authoritative teacher here. Theologians are discovering a more profound sense of what *living* tradition is. One has only to glance at publishers' catalogues to see how extensive is the modern literature on the subject.

VOTES AND CONSULTATION

The *Decree* seems to envisage two ways in which the subjects in a religious institute can make the contribution which is expected of them. One is by means of their votes, the other is in response to consultation.

Neither the *Decree* on the renewal of religious life nor the *Norms* for its implementation assert in as many words that religious should cast their votes for those best qualified to shape and implement the program of renewal, but this would seem to follow necessarily from what the two documents say. If the responsibility for renewal falls on an entire religious institute (*Decree*, par. 4), and if it falls

[5]"Evolution in the Church" in *Supplement to Doctrine and Life* (n. 18), p. 28.

especially on the superiors and general chapters, *and* if I as a subject have the responsibility of electing a superior or the members of a chapter, then loyalty to the Church and to my religious institute demand that I vote for those best able to carry out this vital program. Their task is akin to founding the institute anew.

The *Norms* (par. 18) repeat the assertion of the *Decree* (par. 14) that "chapter and councils should express, each at its own level, the involvement and the concern of all the members of the community for the good of the whole"; and it adds: "This will be the case, especially if the members have a real and effective part in the choice of chapter and council officials."

While both the *Decree* and the *Norms* state quite clearly that superiors are bound to consult their subjects when forming programs of renewal, neither document offers directives as to how this should be done. The *Decree* merely says that superiors, "in matters which concern the destiny of an entire institute, should find appropriate means of consulting their subjects and of hearing their views" (par. 4). The *Norms* say that each institute must call a special chapter within two or three years and that, "in preparation for this chapter, the general council must arrange, by some suitable means, for an ample and free consultation of all the subjects. The results of this consultation should be made available in good time so as to guide and assist the work of the chapter. The consultation may be done at the level of conventual or provincial chapters, by sending out questionnaires, setting up commissions, etc." (par. 4).

One notes that the documents rightly leave it to the individual institutes to discover the most suitable method of consulting their members. The only stipulation they make is that it should be "ample and free." While this is important, one feels that there is need to stress another point of capital importance for all religious at this juncture: the need for study and discussion. If the members of a religious institute are unfamiliar with the letter and spirit of the Council, if they have given no thought to the purpose and role of their institute in the modern world, if they are ignorant of the principles which should guide renewal and adaptation, how relevant will their voting be and how helpful their response to consultation? Subjects ought not to shuffle their responsibilities on to their superiors. All religious must realize that—at this present juncture as never before—the future of their institutes lies in their hands.

Not only are study and discussion necessary for the proper guidance of programs of renewal and adaptation, they can also have a most beneficial side effect: the reassurance of those who are psychologically less attuned to change. Older people tend to dislike change, good or bad, and the *Norms* (par. 10) makes particular reference to "the psychology of enclosed communities, for they have a special need of stability and security." Knowledge and amicable discussion can do much to dispel the fears that beset some people, and which to a certain extent are fears of the unknown. It goes without saying that, in such matters, the older have a special claim on the charity of the young and more adventurous.

The importance of study is recognized both in the *Decree* and in the *Norms*. In fact, the *Norms* give the outline of a course of study in paragraphs 15 and 16. Paragraph 15 refers religious not only to the decree *Perfectae and Caritatis,* but also to "other conciliar documents, especially chapters five and six of the dogmatic constitution *Lumen Genitum.*" Paragraph 16 goes on to prescribe study of the Scriptures by all religious, involvement in the life and mystery of the

Church (because religious life must be ecclesial), the examination and exposition of the "doctrine of religious life under all its aspects (theological, historical, canonical, etc.)" and a "genuine understanding" of the original spirit of their religious institute.

It goes without saying that all religious will not have equal competence in these different spheres; in fact many religious will feel that they have very little competence in any of them. However, it would be a great pity if religious were to refrain from making their proper contributions, either out of false modesty or out of apathy. For, in any institute, the success of the *aggiornamento* will depend on the measure and the extent of the cooperation given by the members. The obligation to study, however, falls particularly on those who have special competence. Thus one suggests, religious who are experts in the Scriptures have a particular responsibility to assist their own brethren, and others, in the formation of a program of renewal. The same applies to theologians, canonists, and historians. Indeed, one knows that many religious institutes have commissioned special studies of points of special importance. One wonders if many general chapters will emulate the Ecumenical Council by appointing experts, *periti,* to attend their sessions and to give lectures on particular points while the chapter is in progress? One imagines that institutes will automatically advert to the need for expert canonical advice in the revision of their constitutions, etc. But the *Decree* and the *Norms* would seem to imply that they have greater need of advice from Scripture scholars, historians, sociologists, etc., at the present juncture. Further, the role of the canonical expert will be different in kind from that of the other experts. The role of the canonist, *qua canonist,* will be simply that of draftsman. It will be for him to formulate in

53

correct legal language the changes in the rules suggested by biblical and theological insights.

However, it is clear from paragraphs 12 and 13 of the *Norms* that, even in the drafting of the constitutions, etc., of an institute, canonical expertise must be supplemented by scriptural and theological expertise. All constitutions, we are told, should contain both "spiritual elements" ("the evangelical and theological principles concerning religious life") and "juridical" elements. Indeed the document seems to visualize the theologian and Scripture scholar looking over the canonist's shoulder when he formulates his juridical sections, and the canonist looking over his colleagues' shoulders as they formulate their portions. For every constitution must be "a combination of both elements, the spiritual and the juridical . . . so as to ensure that the principal codes of each institute will have a solid foundation and will be permeated by a spirit which is authentic and a law which is alive (*verus spiritus et norma vitalis*). Care must be taken to produce a text which is neither purely juridical nor merely hortatory" (par. 13). It is the *Decree,* however, which sets out most clearly and in perspective the sources from which an institute must quarry, as it were, the principles to guide its renewal and adaptations. They are the Scriptures, the inspiration of the founder and the modern world (see par. 2).

It is instructive to note that the *Decree* states the need for a *constant* return to the sources on the part of a religious institute. This is especially true of the Scripture, and the *Decree* emphasizes that religious should "have the Scriptures in their hands daily so that they might know the surpassing worth of knowing Christ Jesus" (par. 6). The *Constitution on Revelation* urges all the Christian faithful, "but especially religious," to read the Scriptures frequently (par. 25). Further, the *Norms* (par. 16) state that "the study and meditation of the Gospel and of the whole of holy Scripture by all religious, from the time of the novitiate, should be more strongly encouraged." The *Decree* and the *Norms*, therefore, are not speaking about an *ad hoc* recourse to the Scriptures, during the present period of *aggiornamento*. They visualize a *constant aggiornamento*, nourished and guided by a constant recourse to the sources.

The object of the constant recourse to the Scriptures is simple and radical: to provide us with a supreme norm: "Since the final norm of the religious is the following of Christ as it is put before us in the Gospel, this must be taken by all institutes as the supreme rule" (par. 2 a). Religious, however, need another norm against which to judge proposed changes or adaptations, the "primitive inspiration" of their founder. One might say that each religious institute has two founders: the holy man or woman who brought it into existence, and Christ. The two are not contrary or even divergent inspirations, for the founder of an institute was but endeavoring to give expression to a particular form of the imitation of Christ. If it were not a genuine form of the imitation of Christ, his institute would not have been approved by the Church.

It was of set purpose that the *Decree* did not use the words "primitive legislation," but "primitive inspiration." Later, the same paragraph speaks of "the spirit and aim of the founder" (par. 2). The point is that the primitive inspiration, or the original spirit and aim of a founder, are not necessarily best expressed, or best achieved, in the twentieth century by laws and structures fashioned in a different century. The distinctions implied here—and they are distinctions of capital importance—are: the distinction between the end and the means to the end; the distinction between a spirit and its incarnation, or between an inspiration and the laws, structures, institutions, in which it finds expression. The end (or purpose) and the spirit (or inspiration), are the constants. What religious have to do at the present juncture—and it is a very delicate operation indeed—is to discover these constants beneath the structures and the laws to which they once gave life, but which may have since, to some extent, become their tomb, having themselves become petrified.

That such an inquiry is no mere academic exercise is shown by the requirement of the *Decree* that "obsolete prescriptions" should be suppressed (par. 3) and by the following more detailed prescription of the *Norms*:

> For the good of the Church, institutes must seek a genuine understanding of their original spirit, so that they will preserve it faithfully when deciding on adaptations, will purify their religious life from alien elements, and will free it from what is obsolete (par. 16 (3)).

> Those elements are to be considered obsolete which do not pertain to the nature and purpose of the institute and which, having lost their meaning and impact, are of no further assistance to religious life (par. 17).

The two passages just quoted describe the operation which the *Decree,* in its original Latin, refers to as *accomodata renovatio,* which is, perhaps, best rendered in English as "up-to-date renewal."[6] It is an operation which aims almost at the refounding of one's institute, but in the spirit of the Gospel and of one's founder. It is almost as if a Dominican were to ask: "If St. Dominic were alive today, how would he reshape the order which he founded in the

[6]This is the rendering suggested by Archbishop Andrew Beck, A.A., of Birmingham, England (*Doctrine and Life,* August, 1965). Archbishop Beck was a member of the conciliar commission on the religious life.

thirteenth century?" If the Dominican were to ask: "What sort of order would he found?" he might get a different answer, but this is not the kind of question the Church is encouraging him to ask. The task of the religious of the present time is to renew and adapt *his own* institute, not to create an entirely new one. If every institute were to attempt to produce an entirely new religious family, the result would be a loss of that variety which the Church prizes. The Church would have twentieth-century institutes, merely, instead of the present colorful variety of institutes as different as the centuries which produced them. The *Decree* reminds us: "It is to the benefit of the Church herself that institutes should have their own proper characters and functions" (par. 2).

In practice, however, the task which the religious of today is being asked to perform will not always be easy. At times he will face well-nigh insoluble problems. The following example may be helpful: one tends to imagine the religious of today in the position of a motoring engineer who is asked to up-date a vintage automobile, of the year 1900. Let us imagine that he has been asked not just to make it fit for the rather special, if not artificial, conditions of a vintage-car rally, but for modern highways. (The religious of today, after all, is being asked to up-date his institute so that it is "in harmony with the present-day physical and psychological conditions of its members . . . with the needs of the apostolate, with the requirements of culture and with social and economic circumstances" [par. 3]). How far does the motoring engineer go with his changes? If he ends up with a sleek, streamlined 1968 model, can he claim to have executed his commission faithfully? Would he be justified in claiming that, if the maker of the 1900 model were alive today, he would reshape his automobile in the same radical fashion? Would it be a justifiable rebuttal of criticism to assert that fidelity to the original maker's "inspiration" meant that one could not replace the automobile with a jet plane or a helicopter, for example? but that one was perfectly in harmony with the original maker's inspiration if one rebuilt his machine into its modern equivalent?

Questions of this sort are not easy to answer. When religious are discussing whether or not a proposed change is a betrayal of the founder's inspiration, or an adaptation guaranteed to give it life in the twentieth century, one hopes that their differing viewpoints will be seen as complementary, rather than as contrary. The fact is that, differing assessments are to be expected. Young people tend to welcome change, good or bad. Older people tend to dislike change, good or bad. Then again, we tend to think in groups. A person who is of a conservative persuasion or temperament will tend to be less receptive to Hans Küng than to Cardinal Ottaviani. Likewise, a progressive will tend to be just as selective in his own way. But it is out of such tensions that progress comes. Only in a morgue can one hope for a complete absence of tension. Differences can be destructive when they become divisive. They can help to construct the future when they are allowed and encouraged to complement one another.

PART TWO:

# The Problems of Contemporary Priests

Augustine Rock, O.P., S.T.D.

# 1: *Spirituality, Status, and Education*

INTRODUCTION

The subject of the lectures, which these somewhat revised essays originally were, was "Contemporary Problems for Priests and Religious." Immediately I was faced with a problem. What do priests and religious have in common that results in their sharing the same problems? It is important that I note in the beginning that I had no intention of considering directly the problems of female religious. They will creep in, of course. Some questions will more or less relate to them in the very nature of things. Also, in some ways female religious are among the contemporary problems for priests and male religious. Having narrowed the matter down, I was still faced with the question of what priests and male religious have in common that results in their having common problems.

Presumably both priests and male religious are human beings. I did not think, however, that I was expected to consider the problems they shared with all mankind. Sexually they are male, but again I did not think the question of falling hair and the choice of shaving soap fell within my province. They are Christian men, but again the field was not sufficiently narrow. Yet it has certainly occurred to you by now that the problems that belong to a human being, those which belong to a male of the species, and those which belong to Christian men do belong to priests and religious in some special way.

61

This raises the notion of totality of vocation. The priest is a priest, the religious is a religious twenty-four hours a day. The priest's heart is treated by the same cardiologist as a movie actor's heart. Yet even here the physician must keep in mind that one man is a priest and the other a movie actor. It is therefore plain that problems that are common to all human beings will sometimes deserve special considerations as they apply to priests or religious.

Since most of those present for the lectures were priests, what I had to say had principally the priest in mind. Very often, *mutandus mutandis,* it referred also to religious. Sometimes I made observations which specifically referred to the manner in which the question at issue seemed to me to affect religious. Many times also a distinction had to be made between the diocesan priest and the religious priest. However, very often it was unnecessary to make the difference explicit.

The priesthood is an office in the Church. Only indirectly is this true of religious profession. I do not intend to go into the question of the vocation beyond this elementary point. The priest is called from among men to do a special work within the Church, a work essential to the Church and essential to the continuation of Christ's presence among men. "And none taketh to himself the honor but one who hath been called by God, as was Aaron" (Heb. 5:4). The priest is called to the priesthood not for his own sanctification but for the sanctification of others. The religious, on the other hand, undertakes to live the religious life, and the Church accepts him to live the religious life, because he is able to do so, and because he has freely chosen to live out his baptismal commitment with more undivided attention than that which, in the nature of things, can be given to it by his fellow Christians. He is a religious principally for his own sanctification. Since we are one body, obviously the sanctity of any member contributes to the welfare of all. Thus indirectly the religious has a role to play in the Church precisely as a religious.

It is not of essential significance to the people of God that this man is a Dominican or a Franciscan or a Jesuit or a Redemptorist. It is not even of essential significance to the people of God that this man is a religious. It is, however, of essential significance that this man is a priest. The practice of a young man newly ordained to the priesthood returning to his home parish to offer solemnly the Eucharistic sacrifice, not only before his relatives and friends, but before that unit of the people of God which is the parish, brings this point out. When the religious takes the habit or pronounces vows, his relatives and close friends try to attend the ceremony to rejoice with their friend that he has taken a step designed to achieve his sanctification. Since, therefore, there is such a tremendous difference between a man's role in the Church as a priest and a man's role in the Church as a religious, obviously there will be many differences in the problems which will arise in his life by reason of these various commitments.

THE PROBLEM OF PRIESTLY SPIRITUALITY

The problem that arises in our time regarding the spirituality of the diocesan clergy cannot be treated together with the problem of the spirituality of the religious, even of the religious who is a priest, in every regard. However, there are many points in which there is a similarity. Even the religious priest, to the extent that he is involved in a pastoral ministry, must adapt the traditional spirituality of the religious life as such and of his particular religious community to the needs of the modern apostolate. This adaptation has been made before in religious communities. Certainly the manner in which Dominican spirituality is lived today by Dominican priests is quite different from the manner in which it was lived in the early days of the Order. In essentials it is much the same, but in many of the very important methods of expression it is quite different. For example, in the early days of the Order the entire Divine Office was sung. It was sung mainly by religious who lived what was essentially a monastic life. They had their times of study and their long periods of silent prayer, but they did not teach school, operate parishes, organize works of the lay apostolate; generally they were not even employed in the organized study and teaching of Sacred Doctrine or in the preaching apostolate. Those who were engaged in these latter occupations, which were the apostolic works then done by the Preaching Friars, were by that very reason dispensed from the obligation of the choral Office.

The idea of a fixed time of meditation would have been incomprehensible to the early fathers of the orders of friars. As a result of the increasing complications of life it became common in religious communities to set aside a half hour or an hour for community meditation, that is, meditation made by each man but made by all at the same time in the chapel. Canon Law does not set down a fixed time for meditation, though it calls upon priests, seminarians, and religious to make meditation each day for a period of time; the term used is *aliquod tempus*. The further changes which have taken place in modern life have forced upon religious and clergy alike the realization of the fact that the mental prayer necessary for the proper orientation and consecration of a pastoral ministry can be and often must be broken up into short periods of time, and must be done according to the times and conditions of life of the various members of the community or of the various individual priests. Another thing, the asceticism of the early fathers was something which modern psychology, the conditions of modern life, and the modern apostolate have tended to revise significantly. Vigils, severe fasting, to say nothing of hair shirts and the use of the discipline, are to a great extent contra-indicated by the needs of the modern apostolate.

It must not be forgotten that the early monks rejected what we know today as an "apostolic purpose." To them the "apostolic life" was a life of retirement from "the world" with full attention to self-discipline, contemplation of the Word of God, prayer.[1] To announce the gospel was the work of those "sent" to do so.

We should also keep in mind the essential difference in the relationship of the religious life and the apostolate as it was understood by the monks and as it is viewed by the friars and later "apostolic" orders. This is especially important for religious women in their process of renewal, since women religious associated with the orders of friars were assigned an essentially monastic life rather than apostolic works. The third order groups established for teaching and other apostolic works (and even some of the more modern congregations) picked up enough of the monastic orientation to try to fit their apostolic works around their prayer life rather than the other way about. The monks taught school, for example, but mainly as something useful to do between the hours of prayer. This mentality partially accounts for the rather ridiculous horarium long observed

[1] A very important contribution to understanding the relationship of the life of prayer to the apostolate in the sense in which we use the term is to be found in M. H. Vicaire, *The Apostolic Life* (Chicago: The Priory Press, 1966). Here the noted historian shows how the idea of the apostolate evolved in the course of the Church's history.

(and sometimes still observed) by teaching and nursing sisters.[2]

As far as the secular clergy is concerned, the changes are even more evident. No real spirituality of the diocesan clergy was developed in the past. The spirituality of the diocesan clergy, like that of the layman, was an adaptation of monastic spirituality. The Council of Trent provided for seminaries for the diocesan clergy, but for the most part it was left up to the religious institutes of the late sixteenth and seventeenth centuries to formulate a spiritual training to be provided in the seminaries for those who would serve as priests of the diocese.

Vatican II has definitively dumped monastic spirituality for the diocesan clergy as it has for the layman. It has established the principle that the clergy should develop a spirituality out of their apostolic work, the pastoral ministry. This presents not only the generic answer to a serious problem of the diocesan clergy as well as of religious priests involved in the pastoral ministry, but it also produces very specific problems.

The specific problems flow from the fact that the whole structure for the development of spirituality is a holdover from another period. The official prayer of the priest, the breviary, is an adaptation of the monastic breviary, designed to be chanted in choir. This fact is recognized, and plans are afoot to do something about it. However, whatever will be done will be done only in a matter of years to come. For the time being the priest is left with the monastic breviary, but the need to use it for a spiritual development that is not in the monastic tradition. Moreover the

[2]An interesting observation is made by J. Hitchcock that the hippies are leaving the "world" at the very moment when Christians are becoming enthralled with it. As we do away with Latin they recite Sanskrit prayers; as we do away with distinctive garbs they adopt them. See "The Christian and the Hippie," *The Christian Century* (August 16, 1967), 1040-42.

spiritual directors that are available to the diocesan priest are, for the most part, men who are themselves trained in the monastic tradition of spiritual life. Even though they may be up-to-date in their reading and study, nevertheless their tendencies will naturally be those they developed in the formation of their own spiritual life. Moreover their reading and study is restricted to the material that is available in this area, and that is inadequate and limited.

Since it is plain, and even officially admitted, that the norms of priestly spirituality are quite inadequate, it has come to be considered quite legitimate to propose alternatives whether one is prepared to do so intelligently or not. With an example set before them of a spirituality strongly mixed with fraud, self-deceit, and pietism, some of the younger clergy have rejected the standards, practices, and methods that customarily have been proposed in the seminary and have eagerly espoused and embraced a pseudo-spirituality which might better be called a social welfare mystique. Since the life of prayer has often been poorly integrated with the actual life and work of the priest, some of these young men question the importance of prayer itself rather than the off-centeredness that has sometimes characterized it. Furthermore, in these days of great emphasis on the importance of the individual, on self-fulfillment, on personality development, on the achievement of individual potentialities, it has become fashionable to devote more attention in the development of priestly character to psychology, sociology, and so forth, than to the formation of genuine Christian motivation and orientation.[3]

[3]Writing in *America* (August 19, 1967), 182, under the nom de plume of Patrick Sanford, a priest says that his answer to the question what a priest is would be that he is a "professional *prophet*." Since he must speak the word of the Lord he must listen to the word. He must study and read the Scripture and, "Above all, he must be a man of prayer, a man who converses with God about the here-and-now relevance of God's word for the people in his care."

## The Problems of Contemporary Priests

In the *Diary of a Country Priest* we find an example of a priest forming his spirituality out of his pastoral ministry. It is thoughtfully developed, but of course provides only suggestions for the American priest of our time. Bernanos insisted that the parish priest needs a special kind of self-sacrifice and powerful courage because for Bernanos a priest must be a man who is unable to compromise. Of course he is right in principle, but one of the great problems of the modern priest is to determine definitively the areas in which compromise is actually impossible. To be uncompromising simply for the sake of being uncompromising is better called stubbornness. A priest should be gifted at the art of compromise in those areas in which a compromise is possible and useful for the work of the apostolate, but he must be a sufficiently good theologian to understand where compromise is impossible.

The great emphasis on personalism in these days tends to obscure the necessity on the part of any well-balanced man of being able to accept himself for what he is, a finite creature. A man must learn to accept himself and God and his relationship to God, as did Bernanos' country priest, who was able finally to abandon himself to the mercy of God and to become reconciled to his own failures.

There is of course a great deal of confusion, indecision, and deep distress as a result of the uncertainty introduced into many areas of morality in these days. Those who are most distressed are those who have always sought to live in the *snug security of detailed regulations,* who have cultivated a "spiritual life" characterized by *safety.* They have never really learned how to transcend the law in a spirit of freedom. Very often even priests retain in their concept of God a great deal of the bureaucratic official who must consult the rule books before coming to a decision. This impression was given to them in their childhood, and not very much was done afterward to eliminate it. Perhaps this very fact brings out the very great problem that many priests, despite the many years of schooling to which they were subjected, have never really developed the habit of thinking about, investigating, and coming to decisions for themselves about their religious commitment.

We may also note that it is largely the result of the form of priestly training common in the past that many priests look upon their priestly office as a function. It follows that they are functionaries of some kind of a bureaucratic organization in which they should advance automatically at a certain rate of speed. As long as they make no mistakes, get into no trouble, give no cause to interfere with their normal advance, they will be promoted in due time. Promotion normally does not depend upon extraordinary competence but simply upon the passage of time coupled with an absence of black marks on the record. Many times the complaints of priests about their circumstances and conditions are really justified, but these complaints are presented simply as *ad hoc* positions. Little effort is made to think through the problem, to get at the real cause and the real remedy.

From another point of view I will consider the difference between prayer and the forms of prayer. Of course we know that the forms of prayer are meant to express and to increase genuine prayer. The priest, however, who views himself as a functionary is very likely to view the recitation of his Office as one of his functions. It is easy for it to act in his life something like a food substitute which is not really food but puts to rest the desire for food. The Divine Office for some is not really prayer, but it allays the "need" to pray. Perhaps without it some would degenerate altogether, but others might be driven to really pray. It is important for the priest to consider his prayer life seriously since his prayer should be relevant to his entire life. Integrity is of the essence of maturity.

Canon Masure makes some excellent observations on the importance of prayer, even of contemplative prayer, in the life of the priest whose spirituality is truly pastoral and active. He notes that the active life requires a secret union with God, and that this is secret sometimes especially in that it is hidden under what seem to be obstacles to it. He notes that the importance of mental prayer must not be over-emphasized, but at the same time that it is essential to any true union with God, since there can be no true union with God without the participation of the intellect.

Some are by temperament especially suited to the active life. Masure notes that it is not necessary to wait for the modern psychologists. St. Thomas Aquinas already recognized that many are unable to prolong cerebration (in the widest sense) without constant recurring contact with action. In the IIa-IIae, q. 182, a. 4 ad 3, he discusses this matter at some length and concludes by saying: "Consequently those who are more adapted to the active life can prepare themselves for the contemplative life by the practice of the active life." Canon Masure says: "It is easy for us to add that, because of the accelerated rhythm of modern life, these contacts with the real must be much more frequent than formerly."[4] He also describes mental prayer as it can be lived even by the most active, and notes that the virtues show up in a special way in the active life. He gives examples, such as the use of wealth in a way that affirms the dignity of man who does not live by bread alone but

[4]*Parish Priest* (South Bend, Ind.: Fides, 1955), pp. 202-3.

needs beauty in his life, but at the same time he needs to preserve a detachment; putting forth great effort but at the same time trusting in God; humility expressed in audacity; supernatural prudence that is not mere caution, but can even appear to be rashness; availability to others as an expression of a true inner union with God.

Obviously, if a priest is to be totally effective in his priesthood, he must be himself a man of holiness, a man of God. The priest is, after all, and it is one of his problems, the living witness to the finitude of man. He is a priest for man. He is for man, but for man in order to refer him to another, "In those things pertaining to God (Heb. 5:1)." Not everyone wants to be reminded that there are "things pertaining to God."

THE PROBLEM OF STATUS

The problem of status is, both intensively and extensively, a very significant one. It is impossible here to consider all of its ramifications, but I wish to reflect briefly upon the problem in itself and then to make some observations concerning the problem as it affects us in our time and in our country.

Priests are men, and men are concerned with where they fit into whatever society happens to be theirs. *The priesthood has no true place in the stratification of human society according to human modes.* We find that, in pagan religions and, indeed, in some Christian churches, the church itself manages to find a place within the civil organization of society to care for the worshiping function of society. This situation affects the clergy to the extent that the clergy are looked upon as a separate class at all. In many pagan religions, where the clergy are definitely a class set apart, they are nevertheless a class which is subject to the civil authority and functions for the civil authority and on its orders. While it cannot simply be said that in all ways and in all manners various Christian churches were or are subject to the state completely and totally (even though the head of the Church is sometimes specifically the ruler of the state), nevertheless, for the most part the church does belong to the state and is subject to it.

The Catholic Church has had its troubles in this regard, sometimes even worse troubles in actual practice than those of some of the separated churches, but nevertheless it was an essentially different problem. In principle it was never accepted that the Catholic Church was subject to the state. As the lay state gathered organization and power, it seemed logical that the protection of the rights of the Church demanded that it gather organization and power to defend itself against the same in the state. Of course it always seemed a very happy elimination of confusion and trouble when both the power of the Church and the power of the state could reside in the same officers. However, the second best thing was to make it perfectly clear which power had the last word. Until the time of Marsilius of Padua there was no serious theoretical contention against the theory of the supremacy of the spiritual. However, in practice, the spiritual very often was subject to the temporal.

In the secular order the tangible benefits of wealth and of authority supported by worldly power could be found. When and where the spiritual authority had vast moral force behind it, the temptation was not so great to depend upon worldly power. It was not worldly power that stood Henry IV at Canossa (1077) in the snow to wait for the absolution of the pope. (At least it was not worldly authority supported by naked power, though the moral power of the papacy must have appeared to Henry to have very

tangible results.) However, when those who wielded spiritual authority fell into moral defects which seriously broke
down their moral authority, they naturally fell back upon
what worldly power they could discover to support an authority which should have depended entirely upon moral
force.

These problems and conflicts are not absent in the
Church today. It might be said that, in our country, the
clergy obviously has no worldly power behind its authority
and therefore there is no particular danger of it relying upon
anything other than the moral force of its divine commission; but the facts are quite other than this. We know perfectly well that politicians, especially in large urban centers,
have long considered the clergy very important in affecting
the distribution of votes and have often sought to be identified with it as much as possible.

Status and the problems directly connected with it are
sociological, and in the effects that they have upon the
individual they are psychological. Material wealth is one
of the elements which contributes to the determination of
status. In this country it is a very important element of
status. However, among the various elements which contribute to status some men are willing to settle for material
wealth even at the cost of the other elements. Therefore it
can be considered separately. However I do not think that
this can be done too easily, and I think that many artificial
results can be drawn from such a distinction. Even those
who seem to settle for economic advantages try to parlay
their economic advantages into a real place in general social
status.

If times are generally hard and the clergy are still eating
well, vocations are no problem. This may sound as if many
youngsters go to the priesthood or to the religious life simply

73

for a roof over their heads and three square meals a day. This is not exactly the case. The very fact that the clergy and religious are eating well in times of great hardship is evidence of the fact that there is a basic respect for them on the part of the faithful, or at least there was such a respect for them late enough to still provide the means for them to go on living. If parents, especially poor parents, see many great opportunities for secular advancement for their children, there is one less reason to encourage them to turn toward the religious life or the priesthood. However, when the priesthood seems an assured living, it can be much encouraged. We see this situation working almost exactly in Spain during the last twenty-five years. The number of vocations are up and down year by year almost in exact proportion to the economic condition of the country. By this I do not mean that the number of religious professions or the number of priestly ordinations will indicate the economic condition, rather it is the number of those who enter especially into pre-seminary schools but also into seminaries and novitiates. This should not seem surprising, distressing, or sordid. It is simply human nature. It is not as if it were a question simply of entering the priesthood or the religious life in order to eat; rather it is a question of finding under adverse economic conditions a lessening of many of the worldly allurements which would otherwise draw away many of those who might have chosen the priesthood or religious life.

The importance of this question of status is illustrated by the reaction of the psychologist to whom David O'Neill showed his theory of the root of priestly problems. O'Neill says of him: "He was inclined to relate the priest's present problems to the sociological change in the priest's status and role."[5] That is, the psychologist was inclined to look upon the sociological changes taking place today as producing something of an Adlerian "power frustration."

Thinking young priests are asking a question very seriously and very eagerly today which many older priests find incomprehensible. Yet I have seen intelligent older priests completely stopped by young priests when they place the question directly to them and demand of them a clear precise answer. The question has arisen and become one of great magnitude: *What precisely is a priest?* One does not run out to check the animals or the crops if everything is going along quite normally. However, when some great change in the weather has suddenly occurred, it becomes a time for re-examination. This is what is happening for the priesthood. This age of tremendous change requires a re-examination of the role which the priest should play. Should the priest seek to find a role proportionately the same (in relation to all the other changes taking place) as that which priests have had in the past? Was this proportionate position so good, so right? Or should we not look much more deeply into what the role of the priest should really be, taking advantage of these changes to cleanse the position and the status which we seek?

The clergy is no longer a class in the medieval sense. It is a class now only as a vocational group. What status, then, does the priest draw from his position as a member of this group? There is a special problem in this regard here in the United States. For many years and up until quite recently the vast majority of Catholics here in the United States were second-rate citizens. They tended to rally around their priests who, generally speaking, were the

[5]David P. O'Neill, *Priestly Celibacy and Maturity* (New York: © Sheed and Ward, Inc., 1965), p. 175.

best educated among them. Because the priest had so much influence within the Catholic community, he soon began to acquire a certain influence outside the Catholic community, more or less as the representative of that community. The Irish advanced in city politics in certain places quite rapidly, more rapidly than they advanced in business and the professions. Since as politicians they depended on the support of their own community and since they themselves had grown up in circumstances in which the priest was the distinguished member of the community, the priest found himself a privileged man in communities dominated by Irish Catholic politicians. Even in places where the Irish politicians did not gain control, those politicians who did, whether Catholic or not, recognized that they had to grant certain special privileges and certain special considerations to the Catholic clergy as a means of gaining Catholic support or at least to avoid the danger of alienating Catholics. Understand here that I am not asserting that at any time the Catholic clergy under circumstances such as those just described were actively able to or ever tried to swing blocks of votes toward or away from any political party. Favors granted the clergy were not specific cases of *quid pro quo*. It was simply a question of showing respect to those the people respected.

Now this is an important point. When Cardinal Mundelein was granted Illinois auto license plate number 1, it was a sign of great respect on the part of the politicians of Illinois for him and for his position. But what is important is this: license plate number 1 on the automobile of the Catholic Archbishop of Chicago was a source of pride to Catholic people generally. They knew that they were discriminated against in many ways; here was evidence that their importance was beginning to be recognized. Soon they would be able to take their place as full-fledged citizens. Now that they have done so there is no particular need any longer for special consideration for their clergy. In other words, the status belonged not to the priest precisely as priest, but to the priest precisely as a symbol of the defensive unity and growing strength of the besieged Catholic community.

Since the priest should be a symbol of the Catholic community not precisely as it is a pressure group but rather as it is the community of love, in his life he should give an example of Christian behavior. This presents a serious dilemma. He must preach the gospel. That means that he must lay out the principles of Christian living and apply these principles generally to the conditions of his times and of the place. This may sometimes win for him the support of the politically powerful and of the wealthy, or it may earn for him their displeasure. When it is necessary to bring such displeasure down upon himself he must do so. But he must avoid the temptation of seeking to win the pleasure of the poor and the underprivileged precisely by baiting those who are in power. This requires great prudence and great dedication to his supernatural mission. It is a temptation to say the things that will cause one to be admired by those who can make life comfortable, by those who can make us feel important and can wine and dine us at the better places. But it is also a temptation, and quite contrary to Christian witness, to assume the role of a rabble rouser.

Yet it is not enough for the priest to say what is right; he must also seek to give an example of doing what is right. For this reason under certain circumstances he must become involved. If he prudently considers it the right thing to do he must become involved in civil rights demonstrations and in anti-war demonstrations. However it seems that it is not right for him to march because he thinks a Roman Catholic priest ought to be in the march, but rather only because he feels that he as a Christian should be in the march. It is unrealistic to say that he marches as a citizen and preaches as a priest. He is a priest when he marches and cannot escape it. Yet priests must themselves understand and must teach the people that, by the specific way in which he considers it necessary for him as a Christian to carry out the things he preaches, he is giving an example of a Christian witness, *but he is not formally asserting that Christian witness must be made in this particular form.* Mary Perkins Ryan gives the example of the good Samaritan whom the Lord cited for his charity, not for his methods of medical practice.

The priest is no longer a man distinguished among his fellow men for his superior education. Very often his education is markedly inferior to that of many of his parishioners. Yet the habit to some extent remains among the clergy, a habit formed in earlier times of acting *as if he were* a man of superior education. He submits himself to the possibility of ridicule in this way.

In the United States material wealth is not only necessary as a means of providing comfort and security but also has a great deal to do with establishing and maintaining status. Since the basic material needs of religious are cared for and since in these days diocesan priests, even those who fall sick or reach old age, are not likely to be left to starve, the question of income and of the use of material things falls, to a considerable extent, under the problem of status.

The diocesan priest presumably did not enter the priesthood to become wealthy, but he did not enter the priesthood with the idea that he would have to depend upon someone's kindness or good will for everything beyond the basic minimum necessities. Although it may seem at first that the religious may simply live poverty according to the standards of his institute, the problem is not quite as easily solved even for him. While the religious priest who works hard occasionally may reasonably enjoy his little bonanzas, he should be able to count on his necessities without difficulty and should be able to adapt easily to having or not having the extras. It is pathetic to see a religious worrying about what his sources of the wherewithal to live the "good life" will be two or three or ten years hence, to take an extended vacation with expensive travel, to live consistently beyond the means normally provided by his institute. It is almost as pathetic in the other direction to see the religious who revels in the wealth and financial prosperity of his community, but is small minded and penurious when dealing with outsiders and is never so delighted as when he can hand over a sum of money to his superior. The vow of poverty is designed to develop and maintain a happy and healthy lack of concern about material things. The diocesan priest, however, has a right to expect some of the reasonable comforts of life and a reasonable security in maintaining them.

People generally desire and expect to see their priests neatly dressed and decently provided for. An occasional luxurious automobile or vacation plan on the part of a priest is not a serious occasion of disturbance or scandal. What is and should be disturbing to the laity, however, is the seeming rivalry among priests in an area to outdo one another in the luxury of their lives. The people also feel, and rightly so, that things are not quite as they should be when the parish provides a standard of housing for the parish priests which is far superior to that of the ordinary people of the parish.

Some parishes are wealthy and some are poor. This is a condition that is not likely to be changed. Obviously a priest in a wealthy parish is going to have more sources of income than a priest in a poor parish. A priest is not assigned to a wealthy parish because he is a particularly effective priest. It is thus simply a matter of chance or conniving or influence that one priest finds himself in a position of financial advantage while another finds himself in considerable poverty. There is much discussion these days of revising the method of reimbursing priests to achieve greater equality. Some of the methods proposed are almost as unreasonable as the extremes that they are meant to erase. A priest studying for a doctorate in religious education at Catholic University recently published an article in *America* which embodied most of the foolishness in a high pitched squeal. He wants to do away with the whole system of mass stipends because it "misrepresents the fruits of the mass, breeds superstition, and leads to such abuses as Mother's Day masses and Purgatorial Societies." He admits that "We may have to wait awhile to recognize how foolish it is to push a wicker basket full of money under the altar and call it the symbol of our spiritual offering." But that a diocese could delay in abolishing mass stipends and reforming priests' salaries "makes one wonder how completely dishonest and out of touch we have become." He thinks priests will no longer desire appointments to richer parishes if free-will offerings are abolished. How this could be done he does not say. He looks for practical universal equality in the remuneration of priests depending upon their years of service, and so forth. He adds: "And no work in the Church is more important than any other." In other words, he wants one more element of advancement to follow simply the passing of years in a priest's life. Surely the priest's initiative should not be especially sharpened by financial remuneration, but it is sheer nonsense to say that no work in the Church is more important than any other. Furthermore it is irrelevant since the importance of the work has little to do with the financial recompense. At the very same time and in the same article he says that "money is a real symbol of man's value of himself and of his work. It can be an extremely important symbol to a man without a wife to encourage him, or an employer who expresses glowing satisfaction." One wonders what world this man is living in, a world in which wives do not push their husbands to make more money and in which the satisfaction of an employer who expresses his satisfaction in ways not reflected in the paycheck is looked upon as more morale building than the consciousness of having helped someone in need.

Perhaps it would be reasonable to discover a way of working out an income tax for priests to be paid into the chancery or into a special fund out of which those in particularly poverty-stricken circumstances could be helped. In this way a certain share of free-will offerings which come to a priest by reason of his being located in a well-to-do parish would be automatically devoted to the welfare of his needier fellow priest. At the same time the principle of free-will offerings is not destroyed; it never could be. Also priests who have special obligations, such as the support of parents, and so forth, could be given some special help in this regard. Standards should rightly be set to curtail extraordinary expressions of extravagance in housing, transportation, and so forth, and on the other hand to set minimum standards that must be met at the other end of the scale.

Finally there is a question of status within the Church itself. As the Vienna report says: "Priests today—somewhat exaggeratedly, but not without considerable truth—think of themselves as 'second class clergymen.'"[6] While bishops today are beginning to call upon particular knowledge from the general know-how of their laity, priests often have little to do with policy making; their task is to carry out decisions made without their participation, much less their consent.

PROBLEMS RELATED TO EDUCATION

A great problem for many contemporary priests is that they were not prepared to be contemporary priests. When I speak of education in this context I do not use it in the widest possible sense of including every environmental factor that influences the development of a man, but on the other hand I do not use it in the narrow sense of schooling. I am thinking mainly of the normal seminary scheme of education which was the preparation for their priesthood of most priests who are actually functioning in the priestly office today. In order to understand the manner in which their education gives rise to problems, we should reflect for a few moments on what priests had ought to know.

The late respected theologian and ecumenist, Father Gustave Weigel, once staunchly maintained that there was no need for parish priests to have studied theology. During a discussion held in 1959 at St. Michael College in Toronto (of which I have a typescript from the tape), Father Weigel compares a seminary to a barber college. He said the purpose of the seminary was to prepare men to perform the pastoral ministry. For the pastoral ministry, he maintained,

[6]"Priest for a New Era," *Cross Currents* (Summer, 1965), 270. Hereafter referred to as "The Vienna Report."

there is no real need for a knowledge of theology. And he claims that very few priests ever acquire such a knowledge, or that any attempt was ever made to teach them theology. To quote his exact words: "All over the world, not strictly in the U.S., the average priest who goes through a seminary is totally innocent of all theology. And this is no criticism of his seminary at all. If only he were to know that this is so and keep his big mouth shut, then we'd be happy."

I have only hearsay knowledge of what is being taught in seminaries today as theology, but perhaps this is all that anyone *could* have, since there is such a variety of things that are actually being taught; it often depends almost entirely on the individual professor. However, most priests who are in the priesthood today were educated in seminaries in which they were taught what was labeled dogmatic and moral theology. Dogmatic theology was generally a collection of propositions which were memorized as true statements of the Catholic faith. These statements ranged from credal propositions to propositions embodying the usual teaching of theologians. Though the distinction is stated some way or another in most textbooks, nevertheless it was never very strongly emphasized. A proposition "offensive to pious ears," or a proposition "theologically certain" was often accepted as being the content of revelation just as if it were *de fide*. This partially accounts for the fact that many priests are deeply shocked today by some of the ideas espoused by the "new theologians." Moral theology was a collection of conclusions hemmed in by an interpretation of the Code of Canon Law. It was generally a collection of negative directives based upon the Ten Commandments. However, even when the division of St. Thomas and the other medieval theologians was used, the positive spirit of that division based on the virtues is often at least partially suppressed.

The point that Father Weigel was trying to make is one that is widely accepted by those seeking to achieve seminary reform today, but they do not say it that way. They talk about "pastoral theology"—which is not theology at all in the sense in which Father Weigel knew it, or in the sense in which St. Thomas Aquinas knew it, or in the sense in which I know it. But whatever it is, it is certainly far more useful to the parish priest than theology in the sense in which the three distinguished theologians just mentioned know it. Almost anything the parish priest knows can be useful to him, and some things are certainly far more useful than others. To the parish priest theology is certainly one of the more useful disciplines, but it is not necessary. Today theology is far more useful to the parish priest than it was ten years ago. The reason is that theology and theological subjects have become common subjects of discussion even in the most unlikely places. For example, articles appeared in recent editions of *Redbook* and of *Playboy* on the "God is Dead" controversy. The parish priest should certainly be able to discuss theological questions at as intelligent a level as the average fairly well-read layman. He should be able to provide a reasonable explanation of the principal teachings of the faith at an intelligent, adult level.

There are many circumstances in which a priest may find himself today in which he would have little or no use for philosophical knowledge. Though not entirely necessary, philosophical knowledge can certainly be very useful in many priestly circumstances. It is safe to say that most priests learned less philosophy in the seminary than they did theology. They had courses labeled philosophy, but generally these courses simply demanded that what were

84

considered to be the principal conclusions of neo-Thomistic philosophy be memorized. Seminarians were not expected to really understand or to penetrate very fully into the process by which these conclusions were arrived at. They were presented with certain propositions supposedly drawn from Kant, Hegel, and others (who would be flabbergasted by most of them) which were neatly refuted in a single devastating line. Today many nuns and some Catholics are talking what they claim is phenomenology or existentialism, and understand enough of what they are talking about to put the priest who is totally ignorant of philosophy at a substantial disadvantage.

What the priest studies under the name of psychology rarely fits him in any way at all to make use of modern psychological knowledge in the development of his own spiritual life, in the direction of others, in the formation and development of human relations, or in the presentation of the message of the gospel.

Sociologists too are showing what their science is able to accomplish and what they are able to provide in formulating and understanding religious problems and in pointing the direction to some solutions. For example, the morning I wrote this I read in the *Toronto Globe and Mail* an article about the results of a sociological survey conducted by Canadian sociologists to determine the prestige attached to various occupations in the minds of Canadians. The justification for such a study pointed out by one of the authors is "the fact that recruitment into different occupations depends to a large extent in a modern society on the social standing which the individual sees in the occupation" (June 13, 1966). Father Fichter, Canon Houtart, Father Andrew Greeley, and others have shown what valuable contributions to the apostolate sociological studies can provide. Obviously the priest will be much helped in his work by some knowledge of modern psychology and sociology.

It has always been recognized by the Church that, before embarking upon philosophical and theological studies, the seminarian should have completed the "liberal arts course." Whatever this may have actually been in practice (and sometimes what that was was rather dismal), in theory it has always been recognized as necessary and it is perhaps more necessary now than ever. For a well-balanced appreciation of the sacred sciences, it is obviously of great importance that a man be a well-educated man.

(The profound study of Sacred Scripture is far more important than it ever was before. It would be possible to argue with this statement by saying that the profound study of Sacred Scripture was always of the utmost importance; it simply was not generally recognized how important it was. There is a certain truth to this; but it is still true to say that it is more necessary today than ever before, because the knowledge of Scripture is more widespread among the laity and every year it is becoming more so; also modern Scripture study has opened the meaning of the Scriptures in a very remarkable way.)

The Council decree on the ministry of priests points out that priests "cannot be of service to men if they remain strangers to the life and conditions of men." Obviously, then, the most learned priest will be quite ineffective in the ministry of the word unless he understands very well the lot in this world of those to whom he ministers. This means that he must make use of every opportunity to investigate the manner of life of business men, professional men, laboring men, women both married and single, housewives and working women, youth—whatever class of people it is to whom he must minister—to understand the conditions in which they live and the problems peculiar to their conditions of life. He can learn much from written studies relating to these various matters, but if his understanding is based only on such studies it will be woefully deficient. He must sufficiently associate with the various classes of people and learn to *listen*, that the words he has read in reports and studies may begin to take life and may stand some tests in the order of experience. The priest is not expected to teach a farmer how to farm or a businessman how to do business, but he is expected to understand something of the world in which the businessman and the farmer must earn their livings, since it is the same world in which they must work out their salvation.

Unfortunately the spirit of study is seldom one of the qualities a young man is likely to form in the seminary. This is not nearly as true today as it was a few years ago. The reason is evident: the vast changes and the form in which new theological and philosophical problems are now put quickens the interest of the seminarian, and of course it is *interest* that produces fruitful study. The priest to whom theological studies were an utter bore and were endured only as a means of passing courses necessary for advancement to the priesthood can profitably try again. He may find that he will be intensely interested in theological problems as they are now presented.

It is difficult to think of any circumstance in which a priest might find himself today in which it would not be necessary for him to devote his attention to study. This need is widely recognized by priests. In many areas, often at the instigation of groups of priests, various types of programs have been developed to help priests to bring their knowledge up to date. Unfortunately this sort of thing is sometimes carried to extremes. It is a common error of our times to think that everything from race prejudice to bad driving can be cured by another course of study. It is not surprising that people widely schooled for the first time should make the same mistake about schooling that the newly rich make about money, namely, that it is the answer to every problem. The clergy, however, are not newly schooled; we should not make such a mistake. We should not make the Socratic error of thinking that if we know what is right we are bound to do what is right. This error has resulted in some places in supplanting the annual retreat with a study week. Important as study weeks are, they are not ordained to the same purpose as the annual retreat and cannot possibly replace it.

The ability of many priests to read has been seriously impaired by the form of their education. The necessity of reading the breviary word by word, syllable by syllable, and the necessity of reading classroom texts in much the same way, puzzling out the meaning of each word, or sometimes committing it to memory word by word, has taken the joy out of reading and has done much to lessen the facility of many priests to read with profit and enjoyment. This impediment can be overcome in varying degrees by a good speed-reading course and sometimes even by a serious attempt to overcome bad reading habits. Today more than ever the priest must read. Would you want a physician in charge of your health whose knowledge of medical developments in the last ten years was confined to a smattering of hearsay picked up in the doctors' lounge in the hospital? Why should any priest think that people would want a priest in charge of their spiritual health who, despite his piety, can only be described as ignorant?

Finally in this context it is of the utmost importance for a priest to be well developed in the arts of communication. How can a priest possibly do justice to the ministry of the word if he is quite unable to express himself with facility either in speech or in writing? Nonexistent talent cannot be created, a flair cannot be produced at will, but the basic art of writing and speaking can be sufficiently well learned to become an effective medium of communication.

STATE OF THEOLOGICAL STUDIES

There is hardly need to note that many changes have taken place in theological studies in recent years. This is neither the time nor the place to analyze precisely what these changes are, but a few observations can be made and should be made to understand the distress that has been produced by these changes in the lives of many priests. We have already seen that what many priests were told in the seminary was theology has about the same relationship to theology as what women's clubs call a "Book Review" bears to reading a book.

Even those who study theology scientifically, perhaps basing their studies on the Summa of St. Thomas and reading extensively in the learned commentators, have had their self-confidence seriously battered by recent theological developments. Such giants of the Second Vatican Council as Karl Rahner and Yves Congar were under a cloud in the Roman schools and were studied and discussed with interest only *sub rosa* in the universities of Europe outside of Rome. Father Colunga was "exiled" from Rome because of an article which he later found quoted extensively word for word in Pius XII's encyclical on Scripture study. The fact that it is perfectly clear now that Congar is a dedicated disciple of St. Thomas Aquinas illustrates how formalized and uncreative so-called Thomism had become. Theology, at least in its presentation, is an art as well as science and wisdom. I cannot resist noting the analogy between what happened to the doctrine of St. Thomas Aquinas and what Haskell says of the later work of Petipa in the Russian Ballet. He says:

> But in every art a period of great perfection gives way to a sterile academism. Raphael and Michelangelo arise, leaving behind both beauty and an impossible path to follow. Their genuine discoveries become laws, the form of their work is followed but not its spirit, and they must await fresh discovery at a later period when criticism allows them to be valued afresh. The formula of their work is followed when its meaning is no more.[7]

The study of the writings of St. Thomas Aquinas is of immense value for deepening one's understanding of the meaning of revelation. However it is not, and St. Thomas himself would have been the first to insist that it is not, a study in itself. To adopt St. Thomas as one's master and guide in philosophical studies is a perfectly reasonable and intelligent thing to do: to carry his role as master to the extreme of taking an oath never to depart from his teaching in philosophy is to destroy philosophy itself. These days Thomistic philosophy (and related scholastic systems) is giving way to an openness to Kant, Hegel, positivism, logical empiricism, and especially phenomenology and existentialism. This broader approach to philosophical study, even when it is made in the best possible way, perhaps especially then, is exceedingly clumsy in its relationship to a scholastically developed theology. A man of genius like Schillebeeckx is able to incorporate phenomenology and Thomistic theology in the formation of new theological development. But it is rather ludicrous to hear some sister or even some en-

[7]Arnold Haskell, *Ballet* (Pelican Book), p. 75.

thusiastic young priest who thinks all theology before Karl
Rahner was, to use Arthur Miller's phrase, "one long amateur
hour," extol with enthusiasm the writings of the really significant contemporary theologians obviously without any
real understanding of what they are writing about. The
amateurs have to a great extent taken over theology, partly
because they have access to the public print by reason of
being professional journalists and writers. The professional
theologian is not willing to indulge in the sensationalism
and irresponsible crowd pleasing that gains for him easy
access to popular journals and crowded lecture halls. An
observation in John Leo's column in *Commonweal* (March
4, 1966) is very significant, perhaps especially because it
appeared in John Leo's column in *Commonweal*:

> Bishop Robert Dwyer of Reno, Nevada, in his syndicated
> column for February 11, offers the opinion that in our recent
> "New Morality" debate (*Commonweal*, January 14), Father
> Herbert McCabe, O.P., got much the worse of the exchange.
> "It is simple honesty," writes the bishop, "to concede that Dr.
> Fletcher is the winner hands down."
>
> We would add that on the basis of mail and the personal
> soundings of editors, it appears that general popular opinion is
> that Dr. Fletcher won the debate, but that among professional
> theologians and philosophers—both Protestants and Catholics—
> the general feeling was that Father McCabe was the winner.

Today many young people, not only seminarians but
laity and religious as well, have the great advantage of
receiving an excellent education. But some youngsters, still
in the years of formal education, are afflicted with out-of-
date teachers. Unless they have prudent and well-read
teachers as well as a spirit of docility, they sometimes acquire the idea that they can discard the learning of the
past and be leaders of the new age without any hard or
serious study. These developments are disturbing to most

priests who are concerned about the truth (theological or philosophical) at all. Of course many priests are not concerned in the least about developments in the intellectual order. They spend their time with children, including adult children, or in managing Church enterprises.

The Catholic press can contribute notably to the general confusion and distress by being quick to publish irresponsible but titillating articles by publicity-seeking theologians and pseudo-theologians, and by quoting statements made by responsible theologians out of context and without the distinctions with which they were made. Of course we must remember that large segments of the Catholic press have long been quite as irresponsible in another direction. Some widely-circulated Catholic papers are still attempting to preserve the triumphalism in which many of us were educated, to see only the successes and glories of the Church in this world. Scandals can be admitted when they have to be, but they are explained by "outside" interference, by the weakness of an individual, and so forth. The stories are reported only if they show the valor, might, and wisdom of the ecclesiastical authorities, and the malice and wickedness of the enemies of the Church. Such papers make honest recognition of the failings of the pilgrim Church difficult and make it a great temptation to sensationalize them. A bad education can be a terrible problem for a priest.

INSECURITY RESULTING FROM EDUCATIONAL DEFICIENCIES
D'Arcy and Kennedy note that the *aggiornamento* has shaken priests profoundly.[8] They refer to good priests, healthy ones. They indicate that the problem of many of these priests is their consciousness of the need to be free, to love,

[8]*The Genius of the Apostolate* (New York: © Sheed and Ward, Inc., 1965), pp. 228 f. Pope Paul VI notes the same. *Cf. L'Osservatore Romano* (September 10, 1966).

and at the same time they wonder how they can realize these needs in the priesthood. Many priests, even among those who had what was always considered a first-rate clerical education, see their education largely evaporate and feel unable to start again. Priests are constantly told that the laity should be doing much of what they now do. If the laity did many of these things at all, they could often do them better. What is left to the priest?

Long before the *aggiornamento* priests had already begun to develop an inferiority complex about their education. Priests (seminary administrators and faculty, chancery officials, pastors—though some of them are sufficiently ignorant to reject out of hand any scientific knowledge—even bishops) are often cowed by a psychiatrist or a Ph.D. in psychology, by one who claims to be a phenomenologist or an existentialist, by a "new theologian." If a priest-psychologist much in vogue says it, especially in a book, it must be so. They are afraid to question it. Priests with some other kind of an education often consider it far more important than their priestly education. A well-known priest who is a psychologist is quoted as saying: "The treatment of serious mental disease is beyond the priest's scope." True enough, but is there not an indication of belittling the priest's "scope" in the use of the word "beyond"? Granted it is not a conscious belittling, but that is not the point. Why not "outside his scope"? The "hyphenated" priests are the ones who "really know something." The priest-psychologist, priest-sociologist, priest-biologist, are all eagerly sought after. And generally those who took their "other studies" in non-Catholic universities are the most sought after of all. There is certainly evidence here of a lack of confidence in the normal studies with which we are equipped to do our priestly work. Perhaps it is a very good thing that there is.

The recognition of these educational deficiencies produces an insecurity which seriously impedes the dialog with those outside the priesthood as well as with other priests. When a priest realizes the unreality of the triumphalism in which he learned his Church history, his apologetics, and a great deal of the rest of what he learned, he is afraid to fall back upon his education in dialog with non-Catholics. He is fortunate if he acquired this fear before he actually attempted such dialog and found himself seriously embarrassed. Greek and Hebrew, indispensable tools for a truly profound study of the Sacred Scripture, are required subjects for advanced degrees in theology. These requirements were normally filled by technically taking a course in each subject. A real workable knowledge of these languages is rarely found even in professional theologians. It can prove a serious embarrassment in dialog with non-Catholic Christians.

Genuine dialog with the educated Catholic laity is also seriously impeded by the deficiencies of the priest's education. It often results in a priest assuming an authoritarian attitude or in simply shying away from serious discussion; sometimes in both. It results in immense dissatisfaction on the part of many of the laity who try to find a priest who can carry on an intelligent conversation, and many simply discount what the priest has to say. This of course impedes the priest's ministry of the word. It takes a priest with justified confidence in his education to steer a balanced path through the theological crises of our times which seem to render nearly everything questionable. The response of some without such confidence is to act as if it were all a flurry in the night which will soon go away; the response of others is to act as if nothing is certain.

Perhaps most serious of all is the impediment to dialog among priests themselves. There is actually very little communication these days between the young and the old in the priesthood, so little in fact that some seem to think that it is a normal situation. The old priest often thinks he has an unshakable principle with which to work and is deeply shocked when he is told, rightly or wrongly, that it is worthless. The young priest is often facile of expression, is "well" read, and payed little attention during his studies to his professors, his texts, traditional theologians, or even the magisterium, but developed a great deal of interest in the kind of reading older priests know little about. He never really had to devote himself to deep, consistent, and orderly study, but his interest resulted in extensive reading of current literature, and wide and constant discussions with his fellow seminarians and others of questions in themselves significant and serious. Seminarians a few years ago would never have discussed such matters outside of official class time, and they were not likely to be raised then. Many of these young men have stored up many isolated ideas and can discuss them with great ease. This I have witnessed time and again in discussions during priests' retreats where older priests constantly ramble on, reminisce, and tell meaningless little stories while younger priests sharply and clearly formulate serious matters that should be intelligently discussed.

In many rectories a tense silence concerning all serious matters of priestly interest, of the apostolate, reigns supreme. The pastor has the authority necessary to effect such a silence, which he does in one of two ways. When he recognizes his deficiencies, and, as is often the case, is convinced that there is nothing to be done about them, either he goes into a shell, refuses to discuss matters, and settles everything by his authority, or else he undertakes a massive and constant bluff. It is hard to tell which approach achieves total frustration in the assistants more quickly. It should be noted here that very often in larger rectories the older assistants side with the pastors, sometimes even surpassing them in intransigence. On the other hand young priests often consider themselves more knowledgeable than they really are. They have read many of the latest books and articles, but they have not read the earlier books which the really good later books presuppose. They often lack self-critical knowledge and the ability and willingness to make distinctions, a condition which can result in a naïve, benighted enthusiasm. And, of course, they lack experience. At the same time we must not forget that sometimes they are driven to aggravating positions by a combination of their youth and their frustration.

Some few attempts are being made here and there to achieve some degree of dialog among priests of various ages and of various educational backgrounds. Where this sort of thing has been handled with great prudence it has often achieved remarkably good results. However, it seems that where it has been attempted it has more often failed. Here the older clergy who possess the reins of authority are principally to blame. Opening matters up to discussion is to rock the boat. Those who have the good seats never want this to happen.

CONCLUSION

Intelligence and the cultivation of intelligence by education produce trouble. The truth shall make you free and freedom is not easy to bear. It requires the exercise of responsibility; it requires the making of decisions; it requires the constant formation of attitudes. A fairly stupid but earnest and goodhearted fellow can get along very well in the priesthood. He will not see many of the problems; he will not suffer many of the frustrations. An intelligent fellow, however, is able to see what is wrong, to see what he can do something about and what he can do nothing about. He may be lazy or lacking in courage and therefore put in the second category what really belongs in the first. However, if he has a reasonable amount of courage and drive, he has an obligation to do what he can about what needs to be done, and what nothing can be done about he should be able to accept with a certain degree of intelligent resignation rather than frustration. Furthermore he must have a good heart, or he is just a troublemaker.

To the extent that a man is Christian he is free; the priest should be an example of responsible Christian freedom. Freedom has no meaning unless it has a purpose. The priest more than other men should understand and appreciate the purpose of Christian freedom. At the same time it is necessary to understand the limitations of freedom. The surest way to destroy human freedom is to pretend that it reaches further than it does. Man's very nature requires that his independence must be limited in order to be real. The destruction of the limitations to human freedom is the destruction of freedom itself. Human liberty exists in a man. Therefore it is subject to the man's own limits, like the white which can be very very white, but there is only as much of it as there is of the tablecloth. The vision of human freedom which is rooted in ignorance, which views human freedom as without limitation, can lead only to frustration and to atheism. It leads to frustration for the same reason that complete Berkeleian idealism would lead to frustration;

it clashes head on with the facts. It leads to atheism, since limitless human independence is incompatible with the existence of God.

The priest must be a living example of the freedom of the Christian man. To be such an example he must understand what he is and his human need of God. He is chosen from among men for the things that pertain to God. He is the living witness to man's needs. Since ignorance is incompatible with freedom, the priest cannot be ignorant. Since he must make decisions, he must deliberately and freely assume attitudes and positions. Since he must exercise responsibility, he must know the facts. For the guidance of his own life he must achieve the greatest depth of understanding of which he is capable. If he is unable to guide his own life, he is useless as a guide to others. But since he is called upon to guide others, his understanding must be greater than would be necessary were he responsible only for the guidance of himself. It is only in the truth that man finds freedom. The priest must know the truth.

# 2: Problems Related to Celibacy

INTRODUCTION

Life's problems cannot be isolated; they cannot be confined merely to one area of life. Here I wish to raise some problems which seem in some special way to be occasioned, aggravated, or caused by celibacy. Some of these problems are merely facets of larger problems, but they are the facets concerned with celibacy. I am not defending or attacking the law of celibacy for the diocesan clergy. I simply accept the fact that it is the law and intend to discuss some of the problems raised by that fact. Certainly I shall say things which can be used as arguments for or against retaining the law, but they are not said for that purpose.

To be fair, two prenotes should be spelled out. One is that those who argue against the preservation of the law of celibacy for the diocesan priest do not necessarily argue against the perfection of consecrated celibacy. However, some deliberately do just that, and others get carried away into doing it at least implicitly. Yet we must remember that it is entirely possible to hold fast to the unquestionable Christian tradition that consecrated celibacy is in itself a better way of life, since more conducive to sanctity, and at the same time sincerely to advocate that it be dropped as a requirement for the priesthood in the Western Church and the Church in the West. The other prenote is that to speak in favor of a less stringent administration of a law is not to speak against the law. As a matter of fact many laws have been saved in principle by temperate administration.

Celibacy is blamed for more than it deserves. Psychologists may argue the point. David P. O'Neill notes toward the end of his book on celibacy that a psychologist to whom he showed the manuscript agreed with him that there is much immaturity and frustration among priests, but he was more inclined to ascribe it to the sociological change in the priest's status and role than to his celibate way of life.[1] I do not think that any one cause can bear all the blame. Here I am merely concerned with some problems of priests to the extent that they seem to be related to his celibate life, his celibate state, and the fact that celibacy is firmly bound by law and tradition to his priestly way of life.

A further qualification to this discussion must be spelled out. There is an immense difference between celibacy as it is vowed by the religious and as it is accepted by the secular cleric. The religious deliberately chose celibate chastity as a way of life; the cleric chose (and was chosen for) the priesthood. Celibacy was a price he had to pay to answer the call he received. This is not to say that he is not called to celibacy. God works through and in his Church; what the Church binds on earth he binds in heaven. The fact that the Church has made celibacy a condition for the reception of sacred orders indicates that those who are truly called to the priesthood are called also to celibacy, but that celibacy is not foremost.

On the other hand celibacy is of the essence of the religious life. The whole of the religious life, therefore, is adjusted to celibacy in ways that the diocesan priesthood is not. The community life is itself designed to give men a sense of fraternity and a mutually strengthening bond. I do not speak so much of the lesser opportunity for tempta-

[1] *Op. cit.*, p. 175.

Problems Related to Celibacy

tion which results from religious community life; I think
rather of the less evident loneliness. At the depths the religious is as lonely as the diocesan priest, but some men
never reach those depths, and even sensitive men touch
them only from time to time. At the surface levels which
affect all the moments of life, the sense of community is
a strong protection for chastity.

One of the elements of the community life is the help
the strong can give the weak. Hardly anyone is weak in
every way, so community life provides a mutual fortification. And those who are strong today may be weak tomorrow. It is interesting to note that St. Cyprian's argument
for lifting the ban against forgiving apostasy was that formerly the Church had given its members the universal example of fortitude; in his time so many had failed that the
Church had to share the fault of the apostate. He saw the
importance to the individual when he is weak (more accurate than to speak of "the weak") of his life in the community, in that case of course the Church itself. Most religious receive, at least to some degree, from their brethren
what they have a right to expect, the fortification of good
example and of fraternal concern. These things are not
wanting to the secular priest, but neither are they available
to him—in the same way, to the same degree, or with the
same consistency.[2]

To fruitfully live a celibate life one must be supported
by a profound spirit of humility and of poverty. As Father
Häring says: "It is unreasonable to renounce married life
if one wills to fill his heart with earthly things and pleas-
ures."[3] Everyone knows that poverty and the spirit of pov-

[2]Cf. Encyclical of Pope Paul VI on Priestly Celibacy, June 24, 1967,
pars. 79-80. Hereafter cited PC.
[3]Address to Conference of Major Superiors of Men given at St. Norbert's
Abbey, De Pere, Wisconsin, July 1. 1965.

101

erty do not always go hand in hand. Sometimes religious can be more avaricious about trifles than lay people are about significant material wealth, and, as Häring notes in the same talk: "If the Institute as a whole is possessive, it contaminates unavoidably also the subjects. . . ." Yet the religious life by nature is ordained to the cultivation of the spirit of poverty and of humility. It is therefore easier for the religious to cultivate such a spirit than it is for the priest whose very secularity involves him in mundane affairs. Leslie Dewart goes so far as to declare celibacy incompatible with the secular priesthood but acceptable in the religious priesthood, since the religious life is peripheral to Christianity.[4] There will be occasion to return to his position later.

Here I wish to recall to your minds the position I already expressed concerning the applicability of what I have to say to priests, diocesan and religious, and to lay religious. I have the secular priest directly in mind; the religious priest and the lay religious must adapt what will be said to their situation. Where such adaptation involves a special problem, if I see that it does I shall try to point it out.

The major part of what I have to say I wish to devote to the problems celibacy raises for priests and religious already committed to it and still professing it. Then I wish to comment on the circumstances for those priests, both secular and regular, who have chosen to depart from their priestly way of life to live with a woman. Finally, I shall make some observations concerning celibacy as it affects those boys and young men who might be called to the priesthood and as it affects those who must accept or reject them and must provide for the formation of candidates.

[4]*Commonweal* (April 22, 1966), 150.

## Problems Related to Celibacy

CELIBACY AND MATURITY

Perhaps the vast majority of people never really grow up. That is an arguable point. Certainly a very good argument can be made for the thesis that it is not uncommon for Americans of adult age, even much schooled (though not very well educated) ones, to be childish in their outlook and in a significant part of their behavior. The caliber of successful television shows and of the apparently effective commercials is pretty good evidence of this. Manifestations of immaturity are probably as common among priests as they are in any other segment of society. However, it is fashionable these days to assume that they are more common, and that celibacy must share a major part of the responsibility for immaturity on the part of priests, that celibacy retards normal personality development, that a celibate cannot be fully human. One of the young priests in Bernanos' *Diary of a Country Priest* (by no means the worst book a priest could use for spiritual reading), which was published in 1936, leaves his priestly life because he finds that it is restricting the full development of his personality, and one of the protagonist's fellow curates in the wretched novel, *The New Priests*,[5] which made a great splash in France in 1964 as a "political tract," took the same course.

Is it true that celibacy is a way of life in which the full development of a mature human personality is notably more difficult and therefore less likely to be achieved than it is for married people?[6] If it could be established that immaturity and pathological personalities were significantly more common among the celibate than among the married this would not necessarily prove any connection between

[5]By M. de Saint Pierre. Published in English translation in 1966 by B. Herder, St. Louis, Mo.
[6]Cf. PC, pars. 53, 56.

celibacy and immaturity. If we narrow the field down to those consecrated to celibacy in the priesthood and the religious life, and if among such celibates evidence of immaturity turned up more often than it does in married people, the burden is even greater of proving that celibacy is the significant factor. It is greater because such a group shares many factors in common, not merely celibacy. But the point to remember here is that nobody has even established the fact that more pathological personalities or more evidence of immaturity is to be found in priests and religious than in married people. *A fortiori* no one has established the role of celibacy in this regard.

In order to live a celibate life intelligently and productively it is necessary that one be mature and balanced. A child of ten is no more a celibate than he is a married man. For him the question has not yet arisen. Celibacy is more than merely the fact of not being married. In the context in which it concerns us it is the permanent resolution not to marry. Religious vow themselves to it because they consider it the more effective way for them of achieving the fullest realization of their potential as redeemed human beings. The cleric who accepted celibacy happily or unhappily must be a mature person if he is to be useful as a priest. But life changes for both the religious and the priest from the time that celibacy was first resolved upon. To go through the various stages of life from young manhood to old age without the normal human relationships of marriage, and to construct a rich and meaningful life without those relationships demands greater maturity than would be demanded for a successful married life. Häring made this point well in the address already cited. He noted that, in the past, a system of protection achieved good external results in preserving celibacy. Today, however, there are many distractions and possibilities of escaping external protection as well as the constant sexual temptations of modern life. "Therefore a much higher psychological, moral, and religious maturity is absolutely necessary."

The problem of maturity for the priest and religious has many aspects and deserves to be considered from more than one point of view. It is raised here by the question of celibacy, but it seems good to give it some consideration beyond the limits of the question which raises it. Man is an integral being; his sexual life cannot be isolated from his total life. It may seem at times that I am wandering somewhat afield. If I am, so be it, but I do not think I can intelligently discuss the problems that celibacy raises without first giving some thought to maturity.

The adult is a man who faces up to reality, the reality of the world in which he must make his life, the reality of himself and of his own relationship to the world with its people. I think a man has made the essential step from childhood to adulthood the day he fully faced up to the fact of his own mortality. Children know that they must die; they know it as the conclusion of a syllogism: All men must die; but I am a man; therefore. As long as a man's acceptance of his own mortality remains at this level he is not facing up to the fullness of the reality. Some men are suddenly brought to the realization that they will die and are never quite the same again. Others who have faced the reality of death in a concrete situation have been able to insulate themselves against habitually accepting it afterwards. Some men do not need to come close to death to fully grasp and accept it as a personal reality. But once it is habitually so accepted, the rest of reality tends to fall into place. A man who cannot forget the temporality of his own life is not likely to pay in permanent coin to achieve objectives which are essentially temporal.

Liégé's criteria of maturity are as good as any and better than most.[7] An adult has outgrown passing enthusiasms and lives by temperate convictions. This does not mean that he is not enthusiastic; it means that he controls his enthusiasm, ordering it to a real and unchanging goal. He thinks out how best to use his freedom and what checks he must place upon himself, lest for an immediate advantage he imperil a long-term purpose. The man who is mature accepts above all the reality of himself. He faces frankly his own motives. He admits to himself why he makes the choices he does, why he thinks the way he does. The adult is fully aware of his social dimension and enters fully into social life. He understands that his purpose and meaning cannot be found in himself alone, but only in his relationship to others. The adult is a man well adjusted to the realities of *his* life.

Particularly when we consider the social nature of man we touch on the supposed need of marriage for the full development of the personality. Like all erroneous ideas that catch on, there is an element of truth in this one. It is true that no man can be fully human without human love, and in marriage human love is normally found in its fullness. (Normally does not mean usually.) This love is expressed sexually in marriage, but the sexual expression is not necessary for human love to contribute all that it should to full and normal personality development. This is clear from the fact that highly satisfactory sexual unions are found between thoroughly immature and irresponsible

[7]See P. A. Liégé, *Consider Christian Maturity*, trans. T. C. Donlan (Chicago: The Priory Press, 1965), pp. 24 f.

people, and from the fact that mature and responsible celibates are not at all unusual.

When a boy enters the seminary long before he has reached maturity, it is essential that healthy human love be a part of his life. I do not say that this is impossible in a seminary milieu, but if it is impossible, or even very difficult, the boy should be allowed to grow up first, then enter upon priestly training. If, for example, a boy has not made satisfactory social adjustments to women and to authority by the time he pulls out of adolescence, he must perform this adolescent task at an age at which people have a right to think of him as a man. This can be embarrassing; it can be dangerous; it can be catastrophic. But if it is not accomplished at all he will go through life a boy in a man's job.

(It should be noted here that there seems to be a kind of dishonesty in the insistence that the minor seminary is needed to provide special studies needed for the priesthood as well as spiritual formation. The only reason for the minor seminary in this country and in these days seems to be the preservation of celibacy.)

It is not enough for a boy as he grows up to have a love relationship with his immediate family. For one thing, he did not discover his mother and father, sisters and brothers; he did not freely choose to offer them his love. Furthermore, he is always something less than fully a man among them, which is one of the reasons why no man is a prophet in his own country. As Kennedy and D'Arcy point out, too close a relationship to his parents can be unhealthy for the seminarian and priest.[8] Family ties can effectively divide a priest's life. As a priest he can remain impersonal,

8*Op. cit.*, p. 215.

aloof, a public figure; as a man he can find his personal satisfaction in his family relationship. In his professional life he is hardly a person at all; he is merely a priest. With his family he is "Joe" who happens to be a priest.

Obviously a priest should love his parents and should visit them as often as the circumstances, their condition, his work, his location, allow. He should enjoy visiting them and be concerned about them, but his visits should be mainly to give *them* joy and comfort. He is in trouble if he finds himself truly comfortable and at ease only with his parents or his brothers and sisters, indeed with those who know him not so much as "Father" but as "Joe" who now happens to be a priest. If he finds human warmth only in those associations, he has a wall around himself as a priest, he is not finding human satisfaction in his priestly work. When his parents are gone, will he not find his life empty? Will he not perhaps look for a substitute that will lead him away from his priestly commitment more than his parents did?

There is also the danger that an emotionally immature priest will enter into relationships in his priestly work more to satisfy his own needs than to serve those to whom he is sent. Such a man plays favorites to the severe detriment of his apostolate. He is the kind of priest who is jealous of the attraction of the people toward other priests, especially of "his people."

This can be a special problem among seminary professors and counselors, particularly those who are young and are still establishing themselves. There is a natural tendency to desire to be thought well of by the students, to be sought out for advice. There is also a strong sympathy for many of the ideas of the students. Often contemporary young people simply "turn off" anyone over thirty. Recently a young seminary professor, very popular with the students, remarked that, if an older priest even implies that he considers them immature, he is immediately "dead" as far as they are concerned. It did not seem to occur to this young professor that it is a serious defect in people of any age to completely reject the possibility of communication with other human beings of any age or class. It did not seem to occur to him that to accept only complete agreement on the part of the other is a rejection of communication. What he seems to be doing is winning cheap popularity by supporting with his superior knowledge the defective attitudes of his students rather than what he should be doing, namely, seeking to moderate such extreme and intransigent positions. He seems to forget that the purpose of a counselor is to render himself unnecessary. On the contrary he is actually seeking to tie these young men to himself, to be satisfying his own emotional needs rather than truly helping those who come to him to attain the independence and security of maturity.[9]

D'Arcy and Kennedy note that recent surveys indicate that one out of two Americans takes his emotional problems in the first instance to a clergyman. The priest differs from other professionals in that he cannot "select" his clientele. Since those who are not particularly attractive people are more likely than others to have emotional problems, and since the priest cannot turn anyone away, this is probably why so many go first to the clergyman. It is also why the priest must be on guard against retreating into "professionalism," using it as a defense against personal involvement in relationships in which no other satisfaction is to be found than that of giving of himself, a satisfaction the immature cannot appreciate.

[9]See *ibid.*, pp. 97 f.

The inability to relate satisfactorily to people is sometimes expressed by shyness, which may be winsome, thus being one of the less unfortunate expressions. It may also be expressed in an authoritarian harshness. Some otherwise wonderful men seriously lessen their effectiveness by a fear of meeting people, a fear which appears at first to be hardness or even meanness. Many people never try a second time.

When a boy is growing up, during his seminary years, serious emotional immaturity can escape the notice of those who are not very perceptive. This is especially true of those who are intellectually gifted and of those with charm. Kennedy and D'Arcy refer to the study of one hundred priests hospitalized for mental (emotional) problems and note that 64 per cent were A or B students.[10] They do not mention what percentage of priests generally were A or B students. Nevertheless it certainly seems to priests with seminary experience that the most astonishing misfits can do very well if they are "brains."

More devastating sometimes, because much less discussed or noticed, is the tragedy of charm. Often the problem began in preschool years. Everyone has experienced the child (of either sex) who can charm the birds from the trees. They don't, but they do charm good grades and all kinds of other advantages, including the right to be thoroughly undisciplined, from teachers, parents, and priests. It is rather sadly amusing to hear the parents of such youngsters bemoan the fact that "he has the teacher wound around his little finger," and at the same time be obvious victims of the same little monster. Such a boy can go through the seminary winning over faculty and fellow students (some see through him, but consider it, probably

[10]See *ibid.*, p. 222.

rightly, quite useless to raise the question), be ordained, and continue to charm all those with whom his relationships are casual. Those, however, who are truly in need of him find him to be empty, selfish, useless. This is no condemnation of charm. Some who have it are deep and real people. But some use it to cloak vacuity. Those who do often find as they grow older that the charm which was accepted in lieu of competence and integrity when all that was at stake were the affairs of childhood is far from enough in the realities of an adult world.

Holy men are men of peace. No matter what turmoil, no matter what pressures they must endure, there is an underlying peace which does not leave them. These days it is called a sense of security. Yet there are levels at which any man is insecure in some ways. No matter how secure a man may be at the level of his confidence in God, there are sure to be areas in which he cannot have confidence in himself. Any adult, however, should have confidence in himself in the establishment and conduct of human relations. He should be reasonably secure in his role as a member of the human family. The man who has a constant emotional need to be reassured that he is understood, who needs recurring evidence that he is liked, such a man is wanting in maturity. A gracious person seeks to please others; an insecure person so needs to please others that he will endure indignities and abandon principles rather than offend. Or he may seek to produce a defense against others, perhaps assuming a brusque, pompous, authoritarian attitude, trading on his "priestly dignity," lest he be forced to communicate at a truly human level.

Many of the problems which seem to be fairly common to priests are symptoms of deeper maladjustments. It is futile to try to treat them at their own level. Without entering into the question of alcoholism as a disease, it is apparent to any experienced priest that some of the most talented among us seem to take to drink. In some cases much time, expense, and genuine charitable concern are expended by superiors and fellow priests in an attempt to turn these men from this habit which at best is wasteful and dissipating. The results are generally disappointing. All the efforts are devoted to attacking a symptom. The real problem remains untouched.

Much the same thing is true of other problems. Consistent and repeated violations of chastity is in itself clearly and evidently an evil. What is not so evident is that, like alcoholism, it is generally an escape from something that runs deeper. There are other problems, not so evidently morally evil and scandalous (though often they are more evil and more scandalous than drink or unchastity), which are also symptoms of much the same fundamental problems which produce alcoholics and men with sexual problems. I might mention marked oversensitiveness to opposition and to criticism, bad personal relationships with other priests (especially those they live with) and with the people, intellectual stagnation manifested in such ways as addiction to television, pathological acquisitiveness (any parish missionary can recount tales of expensive, dust-covered gadgets to be found in rectories), and excessive recreation such as golf, spectator sports, hobbies, movies, purely recreational visiting, detective stories, and many others.

Priests with such problems are often so imperceptive that they do not realize that they have a problem. Their real problem is often simply that they have never discovered who they are. They are empty, aimless, and sometimes frustrated men whose personalities have never sufficiently developed to provide them with a true identity. They try to escape from their emptiness in liquor or recreational activities. They seek the momentary release from the tensions of frustration which sexual satisfaction provides. Or perhaps they seek the boost to their flagging ego which sexual conquest seems to offer.

Here I should mention that these matters are not to be oversimplified. These points are not offered with smug confidence in their universal applicability. As an example of what I mean, let me offer the suggestion that a healthy, normal celibate may need a day on the golf course to release the tensions which a married man would release in sexually expressing his love for his wife. Tension and frustration are not pathological conditions; they are part of a normal adult life. They can be pathological but are by no means always so.

To return to a suggestion of the underlying problems of priests whose surface difficulties are easily recognized, let me consider those who are oversensitive. Some priests seem to think that the slightest opposition is unendurable, that any criticism of what they say or do must be malicious. Others fear that opposition or criticism is a sure indication that they are on the wrong track; they have little confidence in their own judgment. They feel that they cannot risk having it examined, nor can they risk having to defend it. They have lived on the pretense that they are something they are not. To support the illusion requires that others be fooled. What others think is of the utmost importance, since their security depends upon it. Thus they are oversensitive to opposition and to criticism and their personal relations are generally bad.

The acquisitive are seeking an identity in things which they do not find in themselves. It is more than a mere desire for status symbols. That sort of thing is to be found among priests and is particularly sad when they seek symbols of a status which should hold no attraction for them. Here, however, we are concerned with a yearning for material things which stems from a forlorn hope that such things can give some meaning to an otherwise empty existence. Even the clerical garb, perhaps especially the clerical garb, is used in this way. It is an old fashioned idea that a good priest is never found without his collar. We remember the old Irish pastor who went fishing in hip boots and clerical vest. With such men the collar was part of the habits of thinking in which they were formed, habits which were part of the institutional mentality to which the Council dealt a death blow. But with such men the collar was not their substitute for personality, their refuge from insecurity.

Either celibacy or marriage demands maturity as a prerequisite. Marriage is not for children; neither is celibacy. Yet a young man at the age for choosing marriage or celibacy, basically mature though he must be, has much depth and richness of personality yet to achieve. Men of worth who have chosen and lived married or celibate lives show clearly that the fullness of human nobility can be attained in either state. Obviously some individual men could attain it only in the married state; perhaps some could attain it only as celibates, but it is absurd to insist that marriage is essential to the development of the personality. History itself gives evidence to the contrary. As Ida F. Görres said: "The image of the Catholic priest is one of the most powerful and magnificent forms of manhood which history has ever known."[11]

Certainly human love is necessary to any man if he would be fully human. Human love does not need marriage

[11]"A Laywoman's View of Priestly Celibacy," *Theology Digest*, St. Louis (Spring, 1966), 59.

to reach its highest perfection, but it is in marriage and through marriage that it is frequently to be found. The mutual attractions that brought man and wife together are nature's impulse toward love. The sexual union is able to overcome threats to the development of that love, and the children they love together as their own promote unselfishness and deepen their love. This is not, however, to say that marriage is the exclusive domain of human love.

Celibacy is indifferent in itself. It is good or bad depending upon why it is embraced. If it is undertaken for selfish reasons it is evil. If, on the other hand, it is undertaken for generous reasons it is undertaken precisely to promote human love. Again to quote Ida Görres:

> Priestly celibacy represents the marriage of Christ with the Church. Thus the priest *lives* a marriage, not in the narrow space of his individual self but on the spiritual level of Christ's marriage with the Church. The essence of marriage is not excluded from his experience; he is not denied all human relations to live solely for a "cause." Fidelity, gentleness, patience, responsibility, spiritual fatherhood, love are the qualities he must build in himself. Not from mere chance do most people call him "Father."[12]

And Father O'Neill says:

> In the total service of Christ's people he [the priest] can find the full development of his manhood. In his warmhearted acceptance of the reality of others, he will be led to the rich qualities of loving tenderness, compassion, and sympathy which he sees in the person of Jesus.[13]

Some, both priests and laypeople, who so freely condemn the preservation of the law of celibacy for secular

[12]*Ibid.*, 57-58.
[13]*Op. cit.*, p. 159.

priests allege that a man needs a wife to be fully a man.[14] It has been said against them that they would have a man marry simply to "use" the woman for the purposes of his own personality development. Surely they do not mean that. In any case the "use" would be mutual; man and wife would contribute to one another's growth. They would grow together. But to what extent would the marriage of a priest be able to be a normal marriage?

It is not uncommon for medical doctors to be very unsatisfactory husbands and fathers. Marriage may seem to do the physician good, but does it do *them* good, is it good for his wife and his children? If not, it is not really good for him either. Odd hours and an extended work day are not the only or even the major impediments to a good home life. The major problem seems to be that the nature of his work involves him deeply in personal problems. He can use up his patience, exhaust his capacity for sympathy on his patients. He may have little of himself left for his family. Many physicians' wives and children seldom see the considerate, warmhearted, friendly man in their husband and father that his patients see. Furthermore, the personal relationship which in the nature of his work exists between himself and his patients prevents him from discussing his work easily with his wife, while at the same time it makes his work intrinsically more interesting to her. Thus their relationship has a special quality which would be highly unsatisfactory to many women and would markedly lessen the effectiveness of the marriage as such for the development of the partner's personality. Perhaps the very obstacle could be turned to advantage; it is my opinion

[14]It might be noted that, if this is true, it is a denial of the Incarnation, whereby the Second Person of the Trinity was made man. If this is the case, is not his celibacy a rejection of that manhood?

that it very often is. But this is merely further evidence that marriage as such is not necessary for achieving human fulfillment. What has been said of the physician is true *a fortiori* of the priest, since the physician becomes involved in a personal relationship with his patient through a concern for physical health, while the priest does so by direct concern for the person as such.

To conclude my discussion of this problem—the relationship of celibacy to maturity—it should be kept in mind that many who fail to mature in the context of celibacy would probably fail to mature in marriage. Even the problem of chastity is a manifestation of immaturity which marriage does not correct. The man whose approach to sex is immature often will be as prone to unchastity in marriage as he is in celibacy. At the same time we must remember that any human way of life gives rise to problems. The married man may be tempted to seek relief from such problems by turning to sexual thoughts and activities outside his marriage. Since, however, he is able to turn to legitimate sexual thoughts and activities, perhaps the immature married man will be less prone to evil ones than the immature celibate for whom all sexual thoughts and activities are outside the realm of virtue.

CELIBACY AND THE ROLE OF THE PRIEST

A host of books and articles have been appearing which question the wisdom of retaining the law requiring celibacy of diocesan priests in the Western Church.[15] Despite the Council's strong reaffirmation of celibacy and the statements which clearly indicate the support of the reigning Pontiff, many consider the matter open to discussion. *The National Catholic Reporter*[16] finds the subject sufficiently

15*Cf.* PC, par. 43.
16See letter by Häring in NCR (July 20, 1966).

titillating to return to it on all possible and on some impossible occasions. It gave the impression that even the famous four hundred assistants (which has resulted, perhaps to the chagrin of some journalists, in an orderly Association of Chicago Priests fully loyal to their Archbishop), who held a "special" clergy conference wanted to open the law of celibacy to discussion. Did calling for "a new look at celibacy" as the NCR put it, or to quote from the statement of the priests themselves, "Celibacy and the priest's relationships with others should be discussed," mean that they considered a change in the law a subject for discussion, or merely that they considered the subject discussable? It does not make a great deal of difference, but it indicates that celibacy is not just taken for granted as it was just a few years ago.

Celibacy is always difficult. It is rendered especially difficult by the fact that its wisdom, its apostolic efficacy, its virtuousness are constantly being called into question. Celibacy has been under attack before. In practice it has been attacked by large segments of the clergy, even the higher clergy, during periods of the Church's history. How difficult it must have been for a simple parish priest to remain faithful to celibacy when his fellow clergy were taking wives in fact or in name with impunity; when even the faithful, instead of respecting his fidelity, took him for a fool. But even in such difficult days there was little effective rejection of clerical celibacy in principle. The Protestant Reformers rejected it in practice and in principle. That very fact strengthened the resolve of those who rejected the Reformers as heretics.

I do not think that there are many priests who, even in their wilder dreams, think that any change in the law of celibacy will affect their own lives. How, then, does the discussion of the subject prove disturbing? It is disturbing because it is much more difficult to make a sacrifice if doubt is cast on the value for which the sacrifice is made.[17] The value of celibacy is being called into question by those whose claim to fidelity to the Church is generally accepted.

The arguments offered against celibacy, in addition to the one we have just considered at length, namely, that it frustrates the development of the personality, center chiefly around the idea that the world has changed, the role of the Church in the world has changed, and therefore the role of the priest has changed. This argument is offered as a reason for doing away with celibacy. It is important to keep in mind that drawbacks to celibacy are not necessarily arguments for doing away with it. Nothing in this world is perfect. It is stupid to shut our eyes to those factors of the most valued and cherished institutions which give rise to problems, since efforts must be made to solve or lessen the impact of the problems. A mother does not reject her baby because he is not yet housebroken; she subscribes to a diaper service or buys a washing machine. I am now briefly considering, however, arguments which are used against clerical celibacy.

It is claimed that the secular priest is alienated by being celibate from the world he is to leaven; that the priest cannot be truly celibate and truly secular at the same time. Moreover, by his celibacy, the priest is cut off from the layman:

> . . . the celibacy of the priesthood, principally that of the pastoral priesthood, perpetuates a serious, intolerable disunity within the Church which may continue to be ignored only at the gravest peril. In fact the burden of proof should really rest

[17]*Cf.* PC, par. 43.

with those who would contest this proposition: that the good of the Church obviously requires the prudently gradual discontinuation of this custom.[18]

Sort of rises to a shriek, doesn't it? The same author does away with the argument of 1 Corinthians 7 by noting that what St. Paul says there is predicated on the assumption that the *parousia* is at hand. Parenthetically we might note that the argument from secularity concludes to priests giving up their exemption from military service. Perhaps the "intolerable disunity within the Church" also demands that we should do away with the priesthood altogether.

O'Neill finds in celibacy the root of most of the modern priest's problems. He does frankly admit, however, that a psychologist to whom he showed his manuscript disagreed with his Freudian sexuality fulfillment theory. "He was inclined to relate the priest's present problems to the sociological change in the priest's status and role."[19]

A layman who suffers from chronic verbal diarrhea speaks of ". . . that unbalanced view of marriage and sex that has somehow persisted in the Church since Augustine." He asserts: "It seems that to attempt to guide married persons without experiencing their world in any existential way is to be irrelevant." In the same article he fumes about the denial of basic human rights to the priest, tells what should be the case "if a priest decides to leave," equates the priesthood with "some class of civil servants," and of course never fails to be relevant. For some mysterious reason married people are able to solve the problems of celibates while celibates remain irrelevant when they speak of marriage.

[18]Leslie Dewart, *Commonweal* (April 22, 1966), 150.
[19]*Op. cit.*, p. 175.

## Problems Related to Celibacy

We should not stop without mention of the sniping at celibacy that comes even from "good Catholics." It is sometimes the habitual complaint of the self-indulgent against those who practice self-denial. The latter tend to activate the guilt feelings, often subconscious, of the former. The practice of self-denial by isolated individuals does not raise a great problem; they can be written off as kooks or saints. It is the habitual self-denial of ordinary men with whom they must daily rub shoulders that is bothersome. A by-product of the complaint against celibacy is carping criticism of self-indulgence in other areas of life on the part of priests as well as gleeful reports of priests who have failed in celibacy. Good married people practice as much or more self-denial than the average priest; they are not the ones who sound the sour notes. But this chorus we always have with us; these days sour notes are much in demand. Good music is for squares.

The discussion of clerical celibacy, though it itself adds to the problem of celibacy, also has a good effect. It forces a consideration of it which if made in a spirit of confidence in the Church can increase our understanding of its role in the life of the priest. As Père Vicaire notes in his wonderful little book on *The Apostolic Life,* to which I have already called attention, there is no better commentary on Holy Scripture than the life of the Church. Those who have confidence in the Church know that she could not live by proposing a way of life not conducive to salvation. The Church's long and spontaneously developed practice of clerical celibacy cannot be lightly written off.

Both the history of the Church and sound theology can show clearly that there is an intimate connection between the celibate life and the office of priesthood. At the same time, of course, we know from the Scripture and the early

121

history of the Church as well as from the practice of tolerating a married clergy in the East that celibacy is not essential to the priesthood. The Church was not born fully developed, and the *aggiornamento* is completely misunderstood by those who think its purpose is to wipe out two thousand years in the life of the Church. The witness of the early Church is of vast importance for understanding what is essential in the divine message, but so is the whole history of the Church. The religious life is not part of the apostolic institution nor is clerical celibacy. But the spirit which produced both is scriptural.

Very early in the history of the Church, celibacy came to be thought of as especially suited to those who held office. The sentiment for celibacy was so strong by 306 A.D. that the Provincial Council of Elvira (Spain) legislated it for deacons and higher orders. Yet by the end of the century there was still widespread rejection of it in practice. Those who have read widely in the history of the Church know that the Church has always held out ideals which came to be observed only gradually. The nonobservance of this decree of Elvira did not prevent the Popes Gregory the Great and Leo the Great from extending the law to cover subdeacons. Though in practice slow to catch on ". . . with the enthusiastic support of all the leading churchmen of the West, especially men like Ambrose, Jerome, and Augustine, *celibacy* was eventually made *obligatory* on all clerics in major orders."[20] After Justinian I (d. 565), bishops in the East were to be chosen from the unmarried clergy, and the Second Synod in Trullo (not ecumenical, strictly Eastern, 692) in Canon 13 rejected the Western law of clerical celibacy.

[20]Bihlmeyer-Tüchle, *Church History* (Westminster, Md.: Newman, 1958), I, p. 304.

In a sense it is true to say, as Ida Görres does, that ". . . it was imposed from above, only at the beginning of the Middle Ages, and for reasons not entirely spiritual."[21] It is also true to cite the I Lateran Council (1123) as making the first strict universal law (the East was in schism) of celibacy, namely, that marriage was invalid for deacons. It was regarded as law in the Western Church for many centuries, though often disobeyed. Keep in mind that the law requiring the daily recitation of the Divine Office dates within the memory of living men, yet for centuries it was regarded as of obligation. We may wonder whether past ages were quite as "legalistic" as some like to suppose.[22]

There is indication in the Scriptures of an association between the celibate ideal and the holding of office in the Church. Schillebeeckx makes this point and backs it up with the connection evident in 1 Timothy 3:2; Titus 1:6; and 1 Timothy 3:12 between the idea of celibacy for the sake of the kingdom of God and those who held office—bishops, priests, and deacons—in the Church. Even widows assigned to a function in the Church were forbidden to remarry (1 Tm. 5:9), while young widows without such a function were advised to remarry (1 Tm. 5:14).[23]

It is impossible to consider the problems of the priesthood in perspective without considering the biblical and theological foundation for the assertion that celibacy is the normal condition of the priesthood. Historically this has been the case, thus the assumption is that it should be so. Let us look briefly at the dogmatic reasons. To do this I refer you to the superb article of E. H. Schillebeeckx,

[21]*Op. cit.*, p. 54.
[22]It is not my purpose here to detail the history of clerical celibacy. Those interested could make no better start than with Hefele-Leclercq, *Histoire des Conciles* (Paris, 1908), II, pp. 1321-48.
[23]See *Marriage* (New York: © Sheed and Ward, Inc., 1965), pp. 204-5.

"Priesthood and Celibacy." I shall simply summarize it here, but I strongly recommend that the article itself be read and reread.[24]

Celibacy is not a moral value. Thus the superiority of celibacy over matrimony does not belong to celibacy in itself but to celibacy "for the sake of the kingdom of Heaven" (Mt. 19:12). It is a matter of a close personal bond to the Lord in apostolic service to the Church, "for my sake, and the gospel's" (Mk. 10:29). Christ was not unmarried for nothing, but for the sake of the kingdom, and a human being can be so completely committed to Jesus as to exclude marriage. This is the *Christological* dimension of celibacy. The *ecclesial* dimension of celibacy is to place oneself fully at the disposal of the Church because of the personal bond with Christ. (Such celibacy performs a social service to married life by pointing to the heart of married life.) *Eschatologically* the celibate expresses the true purpose of Christian life, that God must be all in all.

The priest is a Christian with the full mission of Christian existence. The priest is sent lovingly by God to men to refer men to something else: ". . . pertaining to God" (Heb. 5:1). This ministry should be experienced as a charism; if not, though valid, it would to a certain extent frustrate the Word and the Sacrament. "In terms of dogma, the priesthood does not in itself require the unmarried state. On the other hand, biblically and dogmatically, a very precise affinity can be perceived between the priesthood and a life of evangelical perfection and, consequently, of religious celibacy."[25] The original call to the Apostles is to "follow him," to "forsake all." "Since serving the kingdom

[24]In *Herder Correspondence* (September-October, 1964), 266-70. *Cf.* also PC, pars. 22-34.
[25]*Ibid.*, 268.

of God through a personal bond with Christ is the meaning of the priestly mission, we get an immediate link with celibacy."[26]

While the vocations to the priesthood and to the religious life are essentially different, there is no essential difference between monastic and priestly celibacy. Priestly celibacy merely for the practical needs of the apostolate could be justified as an individual choice, but not as a general condition; the only compelling reason is for the sake of the kingdom of God. If the free choice of the priesthood does not include the free choice of celibacy, the priestly vocation is deficient, and all kinds of frustrations will result. Celibacy is not imposed from above; the hierarchy freely chooses its collaborators, and it has determined to choose them from among the celibate. This choice, for the reasons given, is in no sense capricious.[27]

There is not a strict demand, but an intimate tendency toward celibacy in the priesthood. The Church could, then, for apostolic reasons, permit exceptions to the general rule, and she now does. Yet it could never encourage uniting the priesthood to the married state, and it would be only in the most extraordinary conditions that those already ordained could be permitted to marry. While the biblical relationship between priesthood and celibacy refers directly to the fullness of the priesthood in the episcopacy, "the objective divine invitation to Christian celibacy will remain essentially bound up with the priesthood, so that we cannot imagine Christ's Church without this element being existentially accepted by many priests."[28]

I cannot imagine any priest who acts in any way as a director to his fellow priests or who is in any way charged

[26]*Ibid.*, 269.
[27]*Cf.* PC, pars. 62, 72.
[28]Schillebeeckx, *art. cit.*, 270.

with the guidance of candidates for the priesthood who would not be significantly more effective in his work for having mastered this excellent article.

## THE BURDEN OF CELIBACY

Celibacy is not in itself virtuous; it is virtuous only when prompted by a virtuous reason. Even then it is important that it be turned right side out; it is a virtue, not a penance. In this sense religious celibacy and priestly celibacy are essentially the same. Yet they differ in a step prior to the conclusion of this line of consideration. A religious takes celibacy upon himself directly and immediately as a means of achieving sanctity. The priest takes celibacy upon himself as part of a package deal, together with his priesthood itself. Since the priesthood is not only taken but conferred, and since the priesthood is not conferred for the sanctification of the priest but rather for the sanctification of the Church, the celibacy of the priest is in order that the people of God might become the kingdom of God. Like the priesthood the celibacy that goes with it is not undertaken directly and immediately for the sanctification of the individual. However, also like the priesthood the celibacy that goes with it must be used for the sanctification of the individual who is the celibate priest. The difference is more in how the priest and the religious came to be celibate than in what his celibacy means to one or the other once it is his way of life.

Celibacy is taken upon himself by the priest or religious for spiritual motives to attain spiritual goals. It is not unreasonable to examine the spiritual life from a psychological, sociological, philosophical, or even biological point of view. But the judgments and determinations made from any of these natural perspectives are bound to be limited and subject to revision in the light of the larger perspectives known only to faith. Arguments against celibacy from natural points of view can often be shown to be conclusions from false or clearly questionable natural theories. Sometimes they can be shown to be founded on highly questionable natural theories; sometimes they can be shown to be founded on highly questionable facts. Often they are merely emotional arguments drawn from unusual (and often fictional) hard luck cases. But we must face the fact that there are also arguments which are exceedingly difficult to answer at the natural level at which they are raised.

Certainly some problems would be solved by eliminating the law of celibacy for the secular clergy. The housekeeper problem is one; but those who start out with a problem and reason to the elimination of celibacy violate elementary logic. They fail to look at the positive values which result from celibacy. Here is an important point. Those who argue from a natural point of view cannot really assess the positive values of celibacy, since the greatest of these values are in the realm of faith. It is no lack of confidence in the creative value of clerical celibacy to admit that it is very difficult, if not impossible, to defend at the natural level. It is most commendable to make such a defense to the extent that it can be made, but the excessive demand for such a defense is another example of the allergy to the supernatural so commonly found in "Catholic" writing, even some theological writing, today.

Father Häring well says: "The primacy of grace is fundamental and must always be in the mind of those consecrated to celibacy."[29] And R. Willmes, S.J., in an *America* review of a laicized French Dominican's book on the need for doing away with the celibacy of the pastoral

[29]De Pere address already cited.

clergy, makes a remark which seems elementary but in these days is really quite perceptive, a remark which could be made of much of the journalistic, pseudo-scientific, and blatantly sensational writing about clerical celibacy which is found these days in journal after journal. "While giving full weight to human considerations of the priesthood, he omits the dimension of friendship with Christ."

For most priests and religious, celibacy is a heavy burden. When I say this, and when any of us give thought to the burden of celibacy, we must keep in mind that for most married people marriage is a heavy burden. In fact, for those who really live it life is a heavy burden. But in what does the burden of celibacy consist? The control of the sexual appetites is quite difficult at some times for most normal men. Such times are generally more frequent during youth, until the late twenties, and again for a few months to a few years about the time that a man realizes that he is not a young man any more, that if he were in mateable circumstances young women would no longer look upon him as a potential mate, that his sexual potency is not very vigorous any longer. This is true of men in any walk of life. A priest has his male vanity. He has made his choice of celibacy and has no intention of going back on that choice, but he does not like to think that he is celibate because no reasonably desirable woman would want him. When he is young his sexual troubles are the result of youthful glandular function, curiosity, spirit of adventure, and the like. When he realizes that he is fast approaching old age he is far more flattered than he formerly was by the interest of an attractive woman. He can be tempted to be less prudent. On the other hand, it is a bit overdramatic to expect the normal celibate man to be constantly suffering temptations of the flesh. A normal man is too busy with his work; a normal priest or religious is too committed to his vocation to have a mind constantly susceptible to sexual temptations. And a mentally healthy man in ripe middle age has developed the ability to laugh at himself; it helps immeasurably to keep in touch with reality.

Celibacy's other burdens are far more weighty and more constant than is the burden of continence. The burden of having to "do for himself" generally falls heavier on the secular priest than it does on the religious, but to some degree it affects both. It is taken very much for granted as the years go on, but it is still a problem getting one's summer clothes out and ready for use, putting the winter ones away, keeping some order about the place, and the numerous other fussy things that can so annoy a man. Married men seldom realize what a nuisance this sort of thing can be to a celibate, and celibates seldom realize how much of this sort of thing married men do not have to bother with. The married man would appreciate his wife more if he did realize, but the celibate is probably better off that he himself does not.

The real burden, however, is loneliness.[30] Some of the spiritual books and conferences on which we were nourished told us that the priest and religious has God for his constant companion and has no reason to be lonely. We know better. God himself said that it is not good for man to be alone, and Adam was created in divine grace. God is pure spirit; man is made to yearn for human companionship. The religious has his community, and both religious and secular priests have their friends, but a man is made to have a wife and children of his own. To a happily married man

[30]*Cf.* PC, pars. 59, 69.

sexual union is a symbol of a much deeper relationship which complements him to the very depths of his being. That is why such a man is little tempted to sexual union with younger and more attractive women—it would be superficial, meaningless; it would be an empty symbol. It is this deep personal relationship that drives out loneliness. It is his own maturing sons and daughters, themselves marrying and bringing forth his grandchildren, that bring a warm sense of human satisfaction to a man as he grows older. These things the celibate may not very consciously miss, but unless he is an insensitive clod he feels their lack in various ways.

As a man thinks more and more of his own death he feels the loneliness more sharply. He knows that some will grieve at his passing, but he will make no real hole in anyone's life. His fellow religious will apportion his still usable goods; the order of religion will change slightly in the monastery; in the refectory his name will be read with the soup course each year on his anniversary. And life will go on. The diocesan priest wonders who will get his parish. He wonders which of the older assistants are keeping a careful, if unobtrusive, watch on his medical reports. One of the advantages of honorable retirement becoming more common and accepted is that an elderly priest no longer has to develop a fatal illness to keep the younger clergy happy. In fact the new pastor will probably be quite solicitous of the pastor emeritus on the theory that few parishes could absorb two *pastores emeriti*. These things have their amusing aspects; if they didn't we could not bear them. It is truly *not good*, not in the plan of God, for man to be alone.

The more sensitive priest will feel these things deeply. Yet he will accept the loneliness as well worth bearing. It is the price of a way of life to which he is deeply devoted, and he has learned to give his love generously and creatively to his fellow priests, to the faithful, especially to those who need him most.

Cardinals Döpfner and Alfrink at the Council listed loneliness as one of the great problems of the priest. It is my opinion that it is, in some ways, his *greatest* problem. Some forms of the priestly apostolate offer much more in the way of natural stimuli to the enkindling of human love than others. Human love has an emotional quality which is stimulated only by human beings. In some circumstances this stimulus is more vital and less dangerous than in others. I once knew a priest who was chaplain at an orphanage for small children. He spent his days at the chancery and looked forward to going home to the youngsters who really needed his very manly love. Some priests, those in large city chanceries, are often an example especially where they form a household with the bishop, have almost no natural stimuli to awaken the emotional qualities of human love in them. Far too often people become "cases" to such priests. They sometimes become rather sad cases themselves.

Psychiatrists and sociologists interested in priests, especially priest psychiatrists and sociologists, do a lot of talking about maturity and love, and so forth. They have a lot of fine things to say, among them that, in the natural order, the kind of love that quickens the spirit is *mutual* love. There can be much mutual love in the priest's life or in the life of the religious. Sometimes there is some danger involved in it, but there are situations in which a certain amount of danger is the price of life. In the admirable essay which forms the introduction to his translation of the letters of Blessed Jordan to Blessed Diana, the late

Father Gerald Vann has two passages which demand to be quoted here.

> Nature abhors a vacuum: terrible things can happen to a man with an empty heart. That is one reason why it can be more difficult for a priest or a religious to be a good Christian, living a really vital Christian life, than for happily married lay people. These can, without too much difficulty, integrate their love of each other into their shared love of God, sanctifying the one and deepening the other.[31]

> . . . his emotional nature, his heart, may be wholly repressed and smothered, the lid firmly screwed down, while all his energies are directed to the avoidance of any wrong-doing, so that he ends in a sort of irreproachable vacuum. (Sometimes this last is justified on the grounds of playing for safety: but safety for what? and at what price?) In the last resort it is better to run the risk of an occasional scandal than to have a monastery—a choir, a refectory, a recreation room—full of dead men. Our Lord did not say, "I am come that ye may have safety, and have it more abundantly." Some of us would indeed give anything to feel safe, about our life in this world as in the next, but we cannot have it both ways: safety or life, we must choose.[32]

The loneliness produces tensions which must be understood and controlled or they may have unfortunate results. It is not only by sexual union that a man's tensions are lessened by a wife. A wife is someone he can growl at, even have a good fight with, and not have to fear that it will imperil the bond between them. When a man suffers injustice or failure at his work, when everything looks bleak, the confidence that he is important to his wife and that she will side with him can restore his spirits. These advantages a priest does not have. If a priest remembers that it is not only himself who does not have this advantage but his fellow priest as well, perhaps a good word at the right time might partially compensate. We can often give one another

[31]*To Heaven with Diana!* (New York: Pantheon, 1960), p. 49.
[32]*Ibid.*, pp. 51-52.

a boost to help get over a shock or to get started again after a nasty blow or a dismal failure.[33]

A SPECIAL PROBLEM

There is a certain *esprit de corps* which is natural to men who are grouped together in the minds of those outside the group. Everyone knows that physicians and lawyers stand up for one another. They do until one of them does something which so obviously disgraces the profession that the very *esprit de corps* requires that he be openly disowned by his peers. This is found in a way among priests as well. It is a mentality similar to that which is found in other professions, in this, that we feel that what one of our number does reflects in a way on us as a group and indirectly on each one of us as an individual. It is somewhat different, however, in that we have more of a personal desire to protect and if possible to restore a failing brother priest, not so much because of what it does to us personally or to the reputation of the priesthood itself, but for the sake of the man who has fallen. Both elements are present, and for both reasons we are interested in the kind of men who enter the priesthood and in their behavior as priests.

The fact of celibacy makes the priesthood and the religious life attractive to certain boys and men with distorted notions of sexuality. Those who are overtly homosexual only in the most unusual circumstances get through to the priesthood. But some whose sexual attitudes are otherwise distorted do get through, sometimes with great ease and success. There are others whose sexual attitudes were not

---

[33]At this point it is a good idea to recall to mind that every coin has two sides. Not every wife is so good a mate, and there are times when no wife is. Furthermore a married man must give of himself when his wife is down and depressed. I think the point of this paragraph is valid, but like all such points it must be kept in perspective. A mentality which always sees the grass as greener in the other fellow's yard is a mentality much too devoted to childish self-pity.

yet formed when they entered the seminary. Sometimes when their notions of sexuality are stabilized it is achieved in an unreal and an unhealthy way as a result of faulty training for celibacy, of distorted ideas of sexuality on the part of those who guided and influenced them, or simply as a result of growing up in the abnormal milieu of the seminary.

This is a fourfold problem. It is a problem from the point of view of the priests whose attitudes toward sex leave much to be desired. It is also a problem for other priests who must deal with them. (This point has been very little considered. I believe it to be of highest importance for the life of the Church, especially in these turbulent times; I think I can show why, and I intend to try.) Thirdly, it is a problem in drawing the open and perceptive young men of today to the priesthood. Finally, it is a problem for the laity, since many troublemaking and just plain foolish ideas are spread by such priests; and it is a problem for other priests, since they have to try to rectify these ideas and forestall their consequences.

Every priest has had to admit at one time or another that "these things happen," because he was unable to cover up for or explain away some fellow priest whose behavior was consistently unjust, selfish, and overbearing, or who was a drunkard, or lazy and self-indulgent, or an out-and-out liar and cheat. Once in a while a priest is exposed as an active homosexual. When this sort of thing happens there is seldom anything to be said, and seldom any occasion on which to say it. Perhaps Father is committed to a mental institution; the civil authorities are generally very happy to dispose of the case in this way, and often enough it is unquestionably the indicated procedure. We need not worry much about such occasional scandals. They happen so rarely that they serve to remind perceptive people that this sort of thing is minimal in the Catholic clergy. We pray for men who are afflicted in this way and thank God there are so few of them. The manner in which the celibacy of the priesthood bears on this problem can be simply stated, but how much and how frequent an effect it has is impossible to say. The continued and almost exclusive association with their own sex through adolescence and early manhood may cause the ten per cent of a youth's sexual psyche that is homosexual to develop while the ninety per cent that is heterosexual remains dormant. Let us not be too quick to condemn some of the experiments with an element of contact with the heterosexual world which are taking place in some seminaries. Enough said of this problem. There is one much worse that demands our attention.

The question I wish to raise now is a delicate one. It has, however, such far-reaching effects on the whole life of the Church and such profound influence on the lives of priests and religious that it is nothing short of criminal to keep it hidden. It is a problem of which history gives evidence whenever the clergy held a distinguished position in society. History gives no direct evidence in the matter; it couldn't. The problem has only come to be clearly definable in the light of modern empirical psychology. Yet there are enough actions, statements, and decisions in the history of the clergy to give strong indication that this problem was present.

Once when teaching a class of sisters I mentioned that, unless something went wrong, it could be expected that better intellects would be found among people with more delicate sense organs. The young sisters jokingly said that they were testing the intellects of one another by pricking each other with pins to see how sensitive they were. In discussing a problem such as this one we must be very careful not to seriously go about pricking each other with pins. It is not as clear as all that. I submit that the problem is there and it is very significant. It should be understood in order that provision may be made to solve it, or at least so that its effects may be mitigated. I can only offer indications; it needs much further study in a spirit of great charity toward individuals and toward the Church.

The problem is that raised by a certain type who is attracted to the priesthood and the religious life largely because it is a dignified and honorable way of living a celibate life. They seldom understand that this is the attractiveness for them of the way of life they are choosing— it is hidden in the depths of their subconscious—or, if they do understand, they look upon the fact of this attraction as a special gift of God by which they are made like unto the angels. Some are latent homosexuals; they have never been sexually stirred by a girl or woman; and their formation in chastity is such that the erotic aspect of their attraction toward their own sex has been deeply buried in their subconscious. Others are better called nonsexuals. Perhaps they are born so; perhaps their formation was abnormal so that their fear of sex has plunged what might have been a perfectly normal sexual mentality into the darkness of the nether regions of their minds. In either case real sexuality is unknown to them.

Ida Görres sees something of this. She quotes a Preface ascribed to Leo the Great for the consecration of a virgin which refers to the dignity of marriage but then speaks of those who turn away from the union of the flesh. The word used is *fastidirent*, which she notes has the implication of distaste, "to turn away with distaste." She notes that the distaste can be the result of repugnance for or fear of sexual union. Secondly, it can denote an attitude toward sex that emphasizes it as a source of confusion, suffering, pain. But the kind of "distaste" that belongs to Christian celibate chastity is neither of these; rather it is a realization of the better way to the goal and is a special gift of God. The Preface says: "To certain souls chosen from among all nations you have given a special gift."[34]

The way in which these nonsexuals are a serious problem is this. When sex is suppressed, a great deal that we do not normally *call* sex is suppressed with it. It is my theory that almost every shred of capacity for genuine concern for others goes with it. A system is soon devised for appearing to be concerned; very early it is evident that society demands this. The system is often so clever that it has, like the wax face on the body of the Little Flower, a vastly more attractive appearance than the real thing. The difference shows up only when it is really tested. Human relationships among these people are generally so superficial that such a testing is not often obvious. They give many more of the small signs of friendship than does the normal man—little gifts that are "so very thoughtful," over-solicitude about the health and prosperity of the friend which is so appreciated, elaborate expressions of friendship. Of course, they love to shop for little things which would have no interest at all for most men; the health and prosperity of the "friend" is important chiefly so that he will remain useful to them. If their friendship were real it would have no need to be labelled. These nonsexual people often appear to be full of compassion for the poor, the suffering, the little ones, but they can turn it off as quickly as they turn it on. It is only for the "image" it creates.

[34]*Op. cit.*, p. 56.

It is important to note that generally these people fool themselves as completely as they fool others. Even more completely, since when the real commitment of themselves which they have so often symbolized is called for and it is not forthcoming, this is obvious to those who were led to expect it and even to bystanders, but not to them. They are oblivious to the disappointment they have created; if it is called to their attention they are indignant, not only that more was expected of them but even that they are not showered with gratitude for the meaningless fluff they offered in place of the self-sacrificing acts of the friendship they had so often symbolized when it cost them nothing. Their indignation is real; it is quite beyond their capacity to give of themselves. They cannot understand what more anyone could expect of them. The symbols they offered were not symbols; they were the reality, all the reality these empty beings have to give.

These people find, in the priesthood, escape from the world in which sex plays a significant role. If they are latent homosexuals, they effectively escape the heterosexual world. If they are nonsexuals, in the normal world they would be like people who do not know a spade from a club and are locked into a hall filled with a bridge tournament. Everyone else is either playing or at least appreciates what those who are playing are doing. Even though they are priests and religious they are in the world; they cannot escape the presence of sex completely. They must take some attitude to it. Some crawl behind their collars and assume an attitude that says, "I know it's there, and I suppose it must be, but it has nothing to do with me, which should make you pleased that not everyone in the world is as sordid as you are." They would not think of tolerating a vulgar word in their presence. Some years ago I read an article in a British medical journal by a doctor who had studied sexual deviates for many years. He remarked that he had great suspicion of a man who shied away from vulgarity. He said: "I have found that a certain amount of vulgarity is a sign of a healthy mind."

Andrew Greeley, on the other hand, calls attention to "one of the minor risks of the celibate life," the priest (or religious) who never outgrew a dirty sophomoric attitude about women. He says that such a man "is harmless really, because he never does anything wrong, but he can be a colossal bore and rather useless as a priest."[35] He might have added (if he had been writing a scientific study; this is a tract for seminarians) that such a man is often covering up a complete lack of attraction to women.

Nonsexuals or latent homosexuals often make "ideal seminarians." Not an ounce of their energy is taken up coping with the normal sexual tensions of a young man. They have a strong instinct for the words and behavior that will please those who can do them good. Since the natural psychological impulses to go out to the other, to give of self, the natural social instincts, simply do not exist in them, they have no trouble with principles, with being true to themselves. Often they are very bright and talented. They give the appearance of being creative—in a harmless, arty sort of a way—but they would never think of advancing a disturbing idea. This would bring wrath down upon them, and wrath they cannot abide. They cannot be identified by appearance in every case, but often they can. They do, however, for the most part make a big thing of neatness. They often have a great yearning for the comforts, the status symbols, the niceties of the "good life," though their in-

[35]*Priests for Tomorrow* (Notre Dame, Ind.: Ave Maria Press, 1964), p. 38.

stinct for self-preservation restrains them from manifesting it too openly too early in their careers. They "learn" what is taught them and give it back letter perfect. They make fine "scholastic" records.

They, and sometimes others, vastly overestimate their spiritual lives. They are smugly tolerant of the lesser breed who find difficulty with prayer. They cannot comprehend difficulties with prayer, since prayer to them is the right words at the right time, the right ceremonies performed, the lamps properly trimmed, the correct vestments clean and neat. They are incapable of loving other human beings, and "He who does not love his brother whom he has seen cannot love God whom he has not seen" (1 Jn. 4:20). The troubles and gropings and disappointments involved in foregoing a genuine love of friendship can make the relationship look a great deal shabbier to those involved and to those who observe, than a nice neat, superficial relationship rooted in utility and governed by a book of rules. Just as they do not *symbolize* their love for other human beings by the gestures of friendship, since to them the gestures *are* friendship, so they do not *symbolize* their relationship to God in ritual; ritual *is* their relationship to God.

Of course, the virtue of chastity is no trouble to them at all. They do not have the virtue because they have no need of it; the matter of the virtue is not part of them. It is not part of an angel either, but angels were made to achieve without it what man can only achieve in a far less perfect way through it. Just as an angel needs no senses or brain to know, so also he does not need the sexual element, the matter which the virtue of chastity controls, to love. But man does.

Since these people often make such a good record in the seminary (perhaps the records are compiled and assessed partially by people whose mentality is much like their own and partially by men who have never had occasion to think along these lines and find no problem with the objects of our consideration), on they go for higher studies. Usually a seminary is blessed with one or two odd-ball professors who are impressed with the fellow who sometimes fails to answer the questions he is asked but asks a probing, disturbing question instead, the fellow who is troubled by the neat, orderly system which he sometimes questions and sometimes ignores, both usually at his peril. And how blessed is a seminary to have one of those strange spiritual directors who appreciates the fellow to whom the life of the spirit is a struggle with successes and failures, but a struggle he is making. He turns out priests, good or not so good—but with faults that are the faults of men. The system turns out its share of machines. And some of the machines come back from Rome (or wherever) to the bishop's curia or the seminary faculty. They minister to the faithful when it is required of them, or when and in a manner that will enhance their reputations as zealous priests. They do not get involved in situations which demand much time and deep anguish of soul unless the situation is one that is likely to come to light to the advantage of their reputations. They brush off the unprepossessing and the uninfluential unless someone is observing to give a report in the right places of their priestly charity.

They are efficient at their desk work, are always ready to do extra work for the bishop or one who ranks between the bishop and themselves; they never question the "little white lies," the self-centered lack of consideration for others, the minor corruption of the chancery. Perhaps they themselves will one day wear the mitre. The man who is not detoured by human sympathy will surely get to Jericho more quickly than sentimental Samaritans.

This condition is present often enough to be a matter of concern for all who love the Church and especially for priests whose work is often affected by chancery decisions, and indeed whose own lives are much determined by them. The bishop who cannot conceive of what a problem with prayer might be, who was never in the least troubled by what he learned or by what he thought about what he learned, the perfect ecclesiastical functionary who is much less disturbed by total unconcern with the two great commandments than he is by infractions of the decalogue, and much less concerned about those (especially if "the good of the Church" requires them) than he is about a misapplication of Canon Law which might embarrass him with the Roman bureaucracy—such a man can be a hard person for a priestly man to deal with.

St. Augustine says in his Rule that the superior should so act as to deserve love rather than fear from his subjects. It is important for bishops and superiors to remember that they can create more unhappiness by the way they do things than by what they do. The man who is missing in his psyche a wheel essential to total humanity may fail to see how anyone could be disturbed by how he does what he does. He can be quite indifferent to the reactions of someone who cannot defend himself. The work of the Church suffers if the morale of priests and religious is low. A railroad president once said to me: "We are well aware of the fact that no railroad management in the world can make trains run on time unless the operating employees want them to run on time."

Two further points should be mentioned briefly in this context. The first is that some problems which are not of the priesthood as such but are often associated with the priesthood are aggravated by, or are even rooted in, the quasi-universal circumstance of the priesthood which is celibacy. I refer to the besetting sin of the clergy throughout history, the lust for power. When a man's lust for power is not moderated by the loving exercise of authority over his wife and children, it can reach absurd proportions; it can wreak havoc in every direction as such a man, if he is gifted with talent, ruthlessly crushes those, be they "friend" or foe, who get in his way. The people in the world are simply part of the world which is to be *used* for his purposes.

This point and the following perhaps do not exactly fit the context here, but they do deserve mention and probably fit here as well as anywhere else. They are applicable to normal as well as to nonsexual men who undertake a life of celibacy. If celibacy does not produce genuine love of God and man, it can turn a man back on himself. It can result in a bitter, self-centered, superficial hypochondriac misfit. He may seem to have a quarrel with anyone who finds happiness or sees anything good about the world. He may be a man who never tires of providing for his comfort and convenience—in major things such as a rectory far beyond the standard of housing normal in the parish, and in minor things such as the times of services and office hours which are inconvenient to the parishioners but convenient to the priest. He may be a man who is constantly concerned about his health, who needs medical and hospital care far beyond what normal people in the parish could possibly afford. Or he may even be a jolly, kindly man, ready to help, but so shallow that his "help" is confined to superficial symptoms of the real problems of those he serves.

This last type deserves a word. They are good men, but their own life experience is so limited that they can think of nothing that spiritual aspirins or bandaids will not cure. They can recommend abstention from sexual relations in marriage, the disciplined practice of rhythm, separation of an invalidly married family, and so forth. Is not this superficiality perhaps the reason so many priests, when they face a real crisis, find it almost impossible to discover among their fellow priests a man sufficiently deep and understanding to serve as a truly valued spiritual director? This superficiality seems to be present often in the most learned and scholarly priests, who can apply their learning to the concrete situations of life only two dimensionally.

To fill out his own experience a man must have much vicarious experience drawn from his understanding association with others as well as from literature and history. To appreciate vicarious experience one must have a definite store of personal experience both horizontally and vertically (both in extent and in depth); one can appreciate another's experience and assimilate it to oneself only to the extent or to the depth that has already been opened within oneself. (Extent—can go in different directions, but no further from the center than one has already gone; depth—no deeper than one has already opened up within oneself. If one has experienced anxiety, another's anxiety can be appreciated though it arise from another source.)

Finally, and this again applies to normal men in the celibate clergy and religious life, though in different ways, as well as to the nonsexual types, we must take note of the distorted notions of sex and marriage that can be occasioned by celibacy.

How, for example, did sexual sins get to be, in the popular mind, the gravest of all sins? Certainly they are not so in the Scripture. Is it not perhaps that they are the kind of sins that the people who "made the rules" did not do? Those who made the rules "endured" chastity; therefore others should realize how great is their virtue. Therefore, pass over easily the injustice, selfishness, neglect of the poor and the destitute, but God help the unchaste.

Even marriage itself can take on an appearance that is badly out of focus. Generally without realizing what they are doing some celibates tend to minimize it. The "relief from concupiscence" notion takes on a prominence it does not deserve, and marriage becomes a remedy for weakness from which they themselves do not suffer. Or perhaps, seriously or ludicrously, the drawbacks to marriage are pitted against the glories of celibacy to make the lot of the married man seem burdensome, degrading, or just a bit silly. It is not impossible that something of a "fox and the grapes" mentality can be discovered here. On the other hand, in the minds of some celibates marriage is over-glamorized, which is just as superficial and unreal.[36]

The *clergy* sometimes, like any special class, tends to make exceptions for itself from the "morality of the herd." Because as a class it assumes certain standards which are especially strict in some areas (particularly those which are most interesting and appealing to the rest of men, such as sex), it expects to be treated with indulgence in other ways. As an institution it defends its exemption from taxes (to the extent that such exemption exists), from military duty, and so forth, on the basis of its consecration to the things of God; but psychologically it expects and gets these

[36]The reaction of some priests to the apostacy of Charles Davis is revealing. The whole thing is easily ascribed to the physical need of a woman. All the rest is malarkey. Rash judgment objectively, but subjectively they can really understand no other factors which could possibly carry much weight. Of course, we must remember that many remarks are made facetiously by men who really know better.

things, at least partially because of its "class morality." Both reasons contribute also to the special treatment often granted clergymen in regard to the observance of traffic laws and to many other courtesies extended to them. This may sound like Nietzsche, but there is the difference that he was advocating a double moral standard which would free the elite from the strictures of herd morality; we are merely noting that in practice something of this exists in regard to the clergy. We do have something in common with Nietzsche; we Christians hold that the law should be transcended, but in a somewhat different sense than that proposed by the creator of "superman."

It should be clear that I think the law of celibacy will always be essentially retained. Its administration has already been somewhat modified; I think it should be further modified. Perhaps the law itself should have some provisions built in to provide in a compassionate way for a situation which has always existed and in the nature of things is bound to exist as a by-product of the requirement of celibacy for ordination. The problem is that of our fellow priests who have in fact taken up life with a woman as if married to her.

Dispensations are granted to religious from the vow of celibate chastity; it has not resulted in wholesale desertion of the religious life. Should dispensations be granted for similar reasons for priests? At first it seems that a simple affirmative reply might be possible. On further consideration, however, we must take the special nature of the priestly vocation into account, as well as the way of life which the secular priesthood demands.

If there is anything clear scripturally about the call to priestly service, it is that the call is to a permanent commitment. It is a call to the service of others; in itself it does not presuppose any particular desire or eagerness on the part of the one called to serve. We have only to recall such examples as that of the Cappadocian Fathers who eagerly sought the monastic life and only with the greatest reluctance accepted the priesthood. Since celibacy is normally included in the call, release from celibacy normally includes the cessation of priestly functions. It can hardly be done easily. Yet it can be done.

If a priest can be reduced to the lay state, *a fortiori* he can be relieved of the obligation of celibacy. It seems clear, therefore, that a reason this release is not readily granted is to lessen the temptation to think in terms of such a release. At first this may seem to be contrary to Christian freedom, and is often claimed to be so. I do not believe it is as simple as that. 1) Christian freedom is freedom *for* something; to be released from a commitment to follow the call of God for the rest of one's life is not what the freedom is for. 2) Psychologically it is much easier to carry a burden from which one knows there is no release than to go on with a mind filled with other possibilities. If things are as they should be, celibacy should not be that kind of an oppressive burden, though from time to time it is. 3) The secular priest's way of life is quite different from that of the religious. The religious has the support of the community and of the other elements of the religious life which the secular priest, in the very nature of his life and work, cannot have. Thus it is to his advantage, and a protection to his freedom, to have the stronger bond of celibacy. (This is a case in which the bond of law protects against enslavement to the passions.)

The difficulty, then, is to find a way to face a situation which does exist with kindness and generosity, but at the same time not to break down reasonable protection for the priest, both the protection we have just noted and another very important kind as well. If it were known that dispensation from priestly celibacy were relatively easy to obtain, some women would be tempted to look upon the priest as a potential husband. That this does not happen often in regard to male religious is perhaps the result of the circumstances in which they live as well as of the type of work they generally do.

Means will surely be found. Some experimentation will be necessary, but it must be undertaken with courage. The numerous priests who, for whatever reason, are now living as married often have obligations that cannot easily be sluffed off, especially if they have children. For other reasons, too, they may have no intention of trying to return to the priestly life, and it is usually better for the Church that they do not. Must they be forever abandoned to the ultimate mercy of God? Is not doing so an implicit request of the Church that God's mercy not be granted? The Church may bind or loose. Should it not find a way to loose when it can? Perhaps regularization of such conditions might be made after a certain lapse of time and after the priest has reached a certain age. In these days the quiet but insistent demand of faithful priests for a solution to this problem can hardly be ignored by those in Rome who often move as if the individual shared with the Church a place in the world until the end of time.

One more point. If some loss occurs as the result of some relaxation such as was just suggested, that loss must not be mourned. A man needs and has a right to some protection of his freedom from the momentary demands of his weakness. He does not need to be walled up against a calm, long-term decision, even if it is a wrong one. Ultimately a man is deprived of the freedom to be right if he has not the freedom to be wrong as well. The Church is not likely to be well served by men who feel trapped in its service.

I have been considering mainly the priest who is already in a quasi-marriage, but it hardly seems that only those who first offend should be able to be dispensed from celibacy. I do not think anything said so far precludes the granting of dispensations to live as laymen and to marry, if such dispensations require a delay of perhaps a year from the time the request is made. Such a delay does not seem unreasonably long, but it might prevent many decisions made in emotional stress.

Finally I wish to raise the question of the effects of celibacy on vocations to the priesthood. In places and times of widespread violation of celibacy the clergy has presented a scandalous image which surely turned many potential candidates away. In these days in the United States we may well ask what kind of an "image" celibacy gives to the priesthood. Does it make it attractive to the young, or does it turn them away? If it turns them away, or if it attracts them, we should ask why.

Does celibacy contribute to making priests the kind of men who win the admiration of the young? It is only one factor in the total "image" the priest presents to the young, and it is difficult to isolate it from its context. Certainly when celibacy "goes wrong" in a man's life, such as in ways already discussed, it is harmful. It might be mentioned here that the effects of a priest on a boy's impression of the priesthood, and especially of the priesthood as a possible way of life for him, depend largely on circumstances. In a small town the boy may know only one or two priests. Almost his whole concept of the priesthood will be formed by one or two men. How those men are talked about by his family and other people of the parish will have almost as much to do with his impressions as the priest himself. In a large city a boy may know many priests, both secular and religious. His admiration for one or two may overcome many bad impressions.

Dating and the preliminaries to marriage begin very early in life these days, and the ideal of celibacy is not promoted today with the same vigor that it once was. Nonetheless most priests and religious are the kind of men celibacy intended to produce. The ideal presented to any reasonable degree in the real order by such priests still appeals to the generosity of the young. The young are still generous, but their generosity will turn to a demanding ideal which seems to them worth realizing. If celibacy, which is certainly demanding, is presented as a means genuinely necessary for the achievement of the priestly purpose it will appeal. That is, of course, provided the priestly purpose is made to appear worth realizing. A difficulty is to be found in the fact that the young today have grown up with so little discipline that they find it very difficult to channel their generosity. Many who come to the seminary and the religious life with the best of intentions find it difficult to bring themselves into conformity with the way of life, even when it is presented in its best form.

When does a young man embrace a celibate life? If he is called to the priesthood, the first and foremost reason is because it is part and parcel of answering the call to the priesthood. As a religious it is part of a total determination to the life of the counsels. Therefore Dr. Baars is talking about the answer to the question when he says: "Psychological studies reveal that, when a man reaches the late middle age, he usually begins to concern himself with more spiritual matters." But of the young man who seeks the priesthood or the religious life, he says: "'In one magnificent gesture he devoted himself to the attainment of spiritual values to which the average man does not feel attracted until much later in life."[37]

The point is well made in the context, but in general the statement would be a little more generous than realistic. Years of experience as a seminary professor and in conducting retreats for priests make it clear to me that many other factors are involved. Dr. Baars was speaking of an ideal situation and would be among the first to recognize that no one with his feet on the ground will be much disillusioned to discover that every young man who enters upon preparation for the priesthood does not do so with the high-mindedness of a Thomas Aquinas.

Young men dream dreams. While their dreams often have a strong element of magnificent love of God and of neighbor, they are well seasoned with romanticism and with personal ambition. The world would be dead if young men did not dream of greatness, and the value system that determines the greatness they dream about is that of young men. Perhaps a Dr. Tom Dooley catches a boy's imagination because he must be close to God, but probably he will appeal to the boy much more directly because Dr. Tom Dooley could know that he had and deserved the admiration of his fellow men in this world.

It is not wrong for young men to think this way; it would be abnormal if they did not. It is not for *wrong* reasons that most young men are drawn to the priesthood and the religious life; it is for *partial* reasons. As a man's life goes on he must adjust his values. If he does not, if as he grows older he does not grow more of a man, his life will become empty; what filled it as a young man no longer fills it as bubbles

[37]*Sex, Love and the Life of the Spirit* (Chicago: The Priory Press, 1966), pp. 65-66.

burst. A middle-aged man's life can look dreadfully forlorn in the perspective of a young man's scheme of values. In the ideal order a man's reasons for continuing to serve as a priest or religious should be better thought out; basically they should be the same as were his reasons for beginning, but they seldom are. Or perhaps they are if we get basic enough.

We are concerned here with motivation toward the priesthood as it is related to the celibacy of the priesthood. A few of the ways in which seminary life attracts unsuitable candidates are mentioned here even though their relationship to celibacy may seem remote. Considered in the light of what I have just said, however, the ways in which this relationship does exist should not need to be spelled out.

In addition to those who have clear defects in their sexual constitutions D'Arcy and Kennedy note that seminary life tends to attract sociopaths who find themselves protected in the seminary from deep and durable human relationships.[38] There are also those who seek in the priesthood status and security which they (probably rightly) think they could never know out of it.[39] While the motive for coming and the motive in later life for remaining may be different, it would be unusual and quite *per accidens* that the later motive would be lacking altogether in the original, or that the later motive would be substantially worthy if the earlier was substantially unworthy.

In view of the requirement of celibacy it is also reasonable to ask whether the definitive determination to live the priestly life is not perhaps required at too early an age. It is argued that a man is often, even normally, com-

[38]*Op. cit.*, p. 223.
[39]*Cf. ibid.*, p. 233.

152

mitted to a lifetime marriage contract by the age at which a man is ordained to the priesthood. The analogy is not, however, very helpful. Would it not perhaps be for the welfare of the Church and of its priests to keep a man for five to ten years in the diaconate, assigned to a parish or to other apostolic work and with the same freedom a young priest now enjoys, before he is permitted to make the irrevocable decision to accept the priesthood? It would be only a partial drawback and would be compensated by other advantages. He would also be subject to further review by ecclesiastical authorities before being permanently enlisted in the ranks of the priesthood.[40]

Would the priest have. fewer problems if he were not required to be celibate? Perhaps he would. He would have still fewer problems if he were not a priest. At least his problems would be of quite a different kind. The relevant question is, rather, whether the problems raised by celibacy are quantitatively and qualitatively sufficient to question the wisdom of the law of celibacy. I think I have made it plain that in my opinion they are not sufficient. That may matter to no one but to me, but it should matter to *any* faithful Catholic that during most of its lifetime, until and including today, it is clearly the position of the Church that the problems raised by celibacy are not sufficient to justify changing the law. Therefore the intelligent Christian thing to do is to try to understand what the problems are and how they can be solved or how their impact can be lessened and above all to try to draw from celibacy all the rich advantage for the life of the Church that it can and should provide.

[40]*Cf.* PC, par. 71.

# 3: The Problem of Authority and Obedience

INTRODUCTION

It is no secret that many priests are confused and demoralized. They are demoralized because they are not accustomed to confusion and do not know how to handle it. The Pope himself has noted this confusion on the part of many priests.[1] It seems far more important that priests should learn to live with confusion and uncertainty than that efforts be made to restore their self-assurance. Self-assurance in these days would border on the ridiculous. It could be achieved only by crawling under a rug.

At the end of the first day of a priests' retreat, the aged and much revered archbishop came to my room to gently note that he feared that I was "disturbing the consciences of the priests." I replied that they had no right to undisturbed consciences in these troubled times. His answer was that they are "simple men." I insisted that they had no right to try to do the office of priesthood in this complex world if they are "simple men." He spent the rest of the retreat gently trying to persuade me to give harmless conferences on devotion to the Sacred Heart. But he did not follow my suggestion to send me home. I finished out that retreat as well as the two more I had come to give. I am very much in favor of deep devotion to the Sacred Heart, but I did not give a conference on it. The archbishop was disappointed in me, but he was very gracious.

[1] Address to Sixteenth Week of Pastoral Aggiornamento, September 9, 1966. Printed in L'Osservatore Romano (September 10, 1966).

Some of the causes of distress have already been discussed. The priest in the modern world has not been prepared to be a priest in the modern world. He has little confidence in his education; this is a very good thing, but it is sad that so little is really being done to help him to rectify its deficiencies. Constant discussion of the value of celibacy and of the problems surrounding freedom and authority are also major factors in troubling the waters. But there is more, and perhaps the real problem is a level or two deeper than the visible disturbance.

A priest is charged with the ministry of the Word, with preaching the gospel. The priest is also the president of the liturgical gathering; it is he who must set the tone and elicit the response from the faithful. Furthermore it is the priest who is charged to act for the Church, judging and forgiving in the sacrament of penance. To do all of these offices he must be a leader of men. Yet those who stand in authority over him often treat him as if he were an irresponsible child. He must be gold on one side and lead on the other, a man before his people and a child before his prelate.

This conflict was not so evident a few years ago. The priest's commitment to the ministry of the Word was not so clear as Vatican II made it. The more archaic forms of the liturgy placed far less of a burden on the priest than does the transitional up-dated liturgy of today. The sacrament of penance required less of its minister when routine was more complacently accepted and the catalogues of sins were less flexible. On the other hand, the areas within which a priest operated with some autonomy were clearly defined, and there was little or no pressure on him to step "out of bounds."

### RESPONSIBILITY OF BOTH SUPERIOR AND SUBJECT

It is easy to blame authority for the conflict; but what is easy is often unrealistic. Authority is held by human beings. Indeed, as Blessed Humbert of the Romans observes in his salty fashion, "The higher one climbs on the ladder, the more one's *pudenda* show." Authority corrupts, especially authority securely held for life. Human beings are constantly struggling to ease their burdens; the human beings who hold authority are no exception. It is far less difficult to rule sheep than it is to rule free men. It is easy for those who hold authority to slip into a subtle (and sometimes not so subtle) attempt to reduce men subject to them to more manageable sheep.

Authorities, however, cannot reduce those subject to them to the level of sheep unless the subjects cooperate.[2] Various methods can be used singly or in combination to obtain this cooperation. Compensation may be offered, such as comfort and security, in exchange for human autonomy. Or it may be made clear that preferment is open to those who bleat and closed to those who speak. And there is always the assurance that true priestly virtue is epitomized in those who are properly submissive to duly constituted authority.

Those who hold authority may be blamed for yielding to the temptation to evade the burdens of their office, but they could not succeed in evading them if their subjects did not yield to the same temptation in another form, the temptation to try to evade the responsibilities of being human. Once a pattern has been set, the man who insists upon acting like a man can be made to appear obstreperous

---

[2] From a somewhat different point of view, Yves Congar makes substantially the same point in *Power and Poverty in the Church* (Baltimore: Helicon, 1964), p. 95.

156

and can be crushed as a trouble maker. What I am saying here will sound to many like an insulting defiance of rightful authority. Many have been so conditioned in their thinking that a matter-of-fact statement to the effect that those who hold authority in the Church as well as anywhere else are subject to a common form of human temptation and often yield to it sounds in their ear like the cry of an anarchist. In such a climate common sense is hard put to survive.

Another way in which authority tends to corrupt those who hold it arises from the temptation to overvalue security. The man with authority often seeks to extend his authority as a means of securing the authority he already has. Once the extended authority seems consolidated the same process is repeated. Thus a man with an area of rightful authority often exercises, together with it, a relatively vast area of usurped authority. Again it could not happen if subjects did not cooperate. And (though it should be obvious let me spell it out) the individual who holds authority due to his particular position generally inherited an already usurped authority together with his rightful authority, and he generally inherited a subject personnel already conditioned in various degrees to sheeplike behavior. A truly great man would seek to correct both defects, but an ordinary man, as most men are, often will not even recognize that anything is other than it should be. *A fortiori* he will hardly try to correct anything.

Certain structural difficulties compound the abuse of authority. The idea that a city should be one diocese was not developed for twentieth-century urban society. In a small diocese with fewer than two hundred priests the bishop may be a fool or a tyrant (or both), but he is able to know his priests and they are able to know him. Few are fools or tyrants, though like most men their personalities may include a smattering of each. Bishops of small dioceses are able to be close to the actual life of the diocese, to the priests and people who make it up. Especially if they have great distances to travel they are accustomed to spend nights in poor rectories. A lot of man-to-man talk, a lot of candor, can come out over a whiskey, a beer, or a cup of coffee in the kitchen before bedtime. The priest of a small diocese may not like the bishop's policies or his decisions, but he has some real knowledge of the bishop as a man. He feels that the bishop either knows him as a man or has deliberately refused to try. The spirit is healthier when it is able to be angry at a man than it is when it is frustrated by an impossible situation.

Many dioceses have grown so large that it is quite impossible for the bishop to know his priests as individuals. Only a few of the priests of the diocese have ever had the experience of sitting down to a leisurely talk with the bishop under favorable circumstances and with no special subject or problem to discuss. The only time most priests of a large diocese ever see the bishop is "on business." Then the priest has the frustration of feeling that all that is known of him is what is contained in his dossier or what has been related to the bishop by a person or persons unknown. Yet that stranger under the purple skull cap is the only one who can make the decisions which will pattern his entire life.

Remedies for this very frustrating situation are being tried. I am inclined to think that they can only partially succeed when they confer genuine authority to act upon a man who can know and be known and who can easily be reached. An "episcopal vicar" without clear authority to make definitive decisions can be more frustrating than dealing with a man known only as "the bishop." The vicar may be a well-known associate, even a personal friend, but if he can do no more than take the matter to an unseen decision maker, all of his ability to listen and all of his sympathetic understanding may be of little worth. It seems that authority in the Church is vested in too few people; its span is much too vast.

In some cases authority is vested in the wrong people. This should scandalize or shock no one. It is true of any human organization. Consensus that the wrong man is in authority is extremely rare. Yet few bishops and superiors are without a significant minority of good men who consider them ill-suited to their position. No American president has ever been able to forget that millions of people considered him the wrong man for the job. What is encouraging and healthy is the gradual development of evidence that the method of selecting bishops can be improved and also that it is possible for a man to outlive his usefulness as a diocesan bishop. Those who are big enough to be able to recognize the latter fact about themselves have much to offer the Church even after their retirement.

The system seems to need some radical revision in the changed circumstances of the times. It makes the healthy exercise of authority impossible in some cases; in others it encourages the abuse of authority. Since authority in the Church is abused,[3] problems will arise from this abuse.

---

[3]This is not to say that the Church is corrupt, or that all authority in the Church is abused, or that authority in the Church is generally abused —it is to say exactly what it says: if you see a foot the shoe fits, put the shoe on; if you do not, you are either remarkably fortunate or you are desperately in need of glasses.

This is as good a place as any to note that there are other important points of view from which this problem of authority can and should be considered. F. W. Dillistone perceptively points to one in his editorial in the July, 1967, issue of *Theology Today*, St. Louis, 132-33, where he indicates that, in his opinion, McLuhan has contributed more than any

These problems will fall in a special way on priests since priests are especially subject to Church authority.

Something should be done about these problems. When considering just what should be done about them we must remember that wherever authority exists among human beings it is bound to be abused. The solution, therefore, only partially lies in attempts to lessen the abuses. It also demands efforts to lessen the effects of abuses when they do take place. A re-examination of the meaning of authority in the Church can be helpful in both ways. I do not intend such a re-examination here beyond noting some recent attempts and expressing my own opinions on the subject strongly enough to make some further remarks intelligible.

First, however, I would like to note a rather ridiculous trend which is being taken seriously by enough people to make it more pathetic than laughable. We know that at the beginning of the Council the great pioneer "liberals" drew many to their side by their kindliness, their learning, their tolerance, and especially their good-humored unwillingness to take themselves too seriously. Now that the pioneering is over, the priests, the religious of both genders, and the laity who take far out "liberal" positions are often little endowed with any of these endearing qualities. They say sensational things which gain them a public hearing far beyond what the value of their ideas deserves. While some liberals are big men, that quality is no longer necessary to be a liberal. On the manner in which authority in

other individual to an understanding of the crisis of authority in the Catholic Church. He says: "The new electronic age with its new techniques of control and its new media of communication brings all existing institutions under judgment. No walls, no palace-guards, no fortifications, no censorship, no sacred languages, can resist the universal operations of these new forces. *Personal* authority is threatened within any large-scale context perhaps as never before. And the small-scale institution can no longer operate independently of the large."

the Church affects priests, some take the illogical and quite unchristian position that priests should be defended against their bishops by civil authority. These people are proposing that, to defend freedom within the Church, the very freedom of the Church itself should be destroyed. Two examples of this muddled thinking appeared in *Look* recently.[4] Nancy McCormick Rambusch is quoted as saying: "Perhaps the American Civil Liberties Union can help them [priests with dissident ideas] someday." And the vastly overexposed and underdeveloped Father DuBay is reported to have said: "The star-chamber proceedings that take place in our chancery offices should be quickly eliminated before they are declared unconstitutional by the American courts."

The temperament of the times cannot be treated lightly. If the Church is to be heard it must speak to real people in terms they really understand. Solemn reaffirmations of the duty of obedience discourage and even disgust not only the indifferent, but to a far greater degree they discourage and disgust good and faithful Catholics. "Today it is the obedient, not the disobedient members of the Church who are confronted with the problem of obedience."[5] Men think now in terms of freedom. Truly thoughtful men think of freedom in the context of responsibility. Above all it is necessary to recognize that human beings are limited beings and as such are unable to sustain limitless freedom. Most of the absurdities surrounding questions of human rights arise from a blind spot concerning human limitations.

True human authority is ordained to the preservation and development of human freedom, not to its destruction. But to understand the role of authority in the Church, it is

[4](February 7, 1967), 26.
[5]Müller, Alois, *Obedience in the Church* (Westminster, Md.: Newman Press, 1966), p. 132.

essential to remember that authority is an analogous rather than a univocal concept. The Church's involvement with temporal affairs from the period immediately following the barbarian invasions through the Middle Ages and into modern times has created a mentality which is inspiring a revolutionary reaction today. Papal and conciliar statements which are part of historical conditions quite different from those of today are part of "theological lore" which makes them difficult to shake off. Theologians were once the greatest plagiarists in the academic world, a world in which plagiarism is a way of life. Until a few years ago the *imprimatur* was almost a solemn declaration that the book to which it was granted was sheer plagiarism. If it said anything original it was suspect. Concepts of Church authority developed to suit a temporal situation the Church probably never should have assumed still cloud some ecclesiastical "thinking" and a great deal of ecclesiastical practice. "Ecclesiastical commands (and we say this advisedly) are hardly ever given in a brotherly spirit."[6]

MCKENZIE

Today authority in the Church is being widely re-examined. To see what the trends are in this re-examination we can look at a few of the more widely circulated and highly regarded attempts. *Authority in the Church*[7] is from the pen of a first-rate Scripture scholar who is not bashful about expressing himself on subjects other than Scripture. It is a good thing that he is not, since he generally has something worthwhile to say, and he says it with clarity and incisive humor. The first part of this 184-page book by John L. McKenzie, S.J., examines the New Testament

[6]*Ibid.*, p. 141.
[7](New York: © Sheed and Ward, Inc., 1966).

for what it has to say about authority in the Church. The
second part consists of "reflections" on the subject. He
holds that authority in the Church is unique; therefore
the obedience owed to it is unique. Church authority is
an authority of service which flows from love. The Church
is not established on the Code of Canon Law but on a common commitment to Jesus Christ who came to do away
with the Law and establish freedom in grace. Law is
necessary, but a law that is to be transcended in freedom
rather than to become a fixation. It is impossible here to
summarize McKenzie's thesis justly, but we can say something of his ideas, with the strong recommendation that
his book be read and pondered.

The remarkable reputation McKenzie has gained for
himself leads some to read him uncritically, which he would
be the first to deplore. Even when he is in his own field
exposing the New Testament teaching on authority he is
gathering and interpreting. Like anyone else he is capable
of reading what he feels into what he sees. How he feels
he makes no attempt to conceal in the second part of the
book. A few quotations:

> All members owe to Jesus Christ in other members the *dia-
> konia* of love; and this duty is laid upon the officers of the
> Church more explicitly than it is laid upon the members. Im-
> position of one's will is a strange form of *diakonia* (p. 112).

> The contrast between the broad commission which Jesus
> gave his Church to proclaim the gospel and the detailed di-
> rections which now exist for the conduct of even the simplest
> organizations within the Church is striking. Parkinson's Law
> operates as well within the Church as it does in secular
> organizations (p. 117).

> Over-management expresses a doubt that the Church re-
> tains the power it has by its constitution of producing a num-

ber of men and women who can initiate, plan, and execute without constant detailed directions from an ecclesiastical officer. Paul had no doubt that the apostolic Church had this power. What has the Church lost since apostolic times? (p. 117)

The security with which he expresses his convictions when he speaks of the Scripture can mislead those of us who are not so sure of our competence in this area. We can be led to place more confidence in his judgments than even he would expect. For example, he says: "If we restrict certain sayings as uttered to the officers of the Church, we introduce a distinction which the Gospels do not make" (p. 34). All he can legitimately mean is that he cannot find it there. Neither can I. Probably he is right, but I am not completely satisfied that the matter is therefore closed.

The problems which arise out of authority and its use and abuse perhaps are partially indicated in the list McKenzie gives of ways in which ecclesiastical authority has been destroying its own prestige. He notes that the greatest blow to such prestige was delivered by John XXIII who projected a new image against which other prelates have been measured, who openly showed his impatience with ecclesiastical bureaucracy and pomp, who plainly indicated that the Church was out of date. McKenzie lists areas in which prestige has been lost:

1) Segregation: American bishops are damned if they do and damned if they don't, but this they brought on themselves by failing to take a firm position years ago.

2) Birth control: He quotes Matthew 23:4: "They bind heavy burdens, hard to bear, and lay them on men's shoulders; but they themselves will not move them with their finger." McKenzie comments: "A thesis which needs re-examination and restatement, they (the victims of the

ironclad thesis) think, should have been presented with more reserve in the first place" (p. 103).

3) The growing awareness of arbitrary and autocratic, even unjust and vindictive, uses of ecclesiastical power.

4) The unhealthy relation of ecclesiastical authority to political authority. "It is still too recent for us to forget the loss of prestige which the Church suffered when this declaration (on religious liberty) was delayed in a previous session" (p. 105). (I should note here that McKenzie surely knows by now that many, both in and out of the Church, consider this delay a great blessing and a manifestation of considerable wisdom.)

5) Ecclesiastical pomp and ceremony.

6) The obvious economic security which permits of such pomp and "on which ecclesiastical authority reposes" (p. 107).

McKenzie observes that these samples "seem to admit no denial" (p. 107). The flavor of his thinking is communicated in the following quotation:

> The argument most frequently alleged in defense of over-management is the duty of officers to protect the Church and its members. . . . Protection which guards the members of the Church as if they were retarded children or chronic invalids protects them, but defeats the purpose of the Church. Protection of the Church against herself is paradoxical. Protection which treats the members as if they were thieving servants or intruders in the Church does little credit either to the members or to the officers. If the reservation of decision to Church officers did assure the protection of the members of the Church, such reservation would still be contrary to the New Testament idea of authority. But experience forbids us to believe that reservation of decision to Church officers does protect; in particular, it fails to protect the members from the officers. Experience shows that the officers of the Church deserve just as much confidence as the members of the Church, no more and no less. And why should the officers deserve more or less confidence? There are different gifts, but the same Spirit (pp. 117-18).

Is there abuse of authority in the Church? Of course. There is abuse of authority anywhere that authority exists. But Church authority is different. McKenzie says it is an analogous concept relative to any other kind of authority. In any case, if it does not proceed from love and elicit a loving response of obedience, there seems to be no point whatever in the use of force of any kind. The Church is to lead men to salvation, not to force them into a goose step. If love does not respond to love, it just isn't the Church: "By this shall men know that you are my disciples, that you have love one for another" (Jn. 13:35).

What I have said of McKenzie's ideas should convey the notion that they deserve very serious consideration. To say that they should not be gulped down uncritically is not intended to belittle them. He is a first-rate scholar, and in matters of opinion he shows balanced judgment. He is very outspoken, but he speaks with manifest love for the Church. It is perfectly clear today that priests and religious are very disturbed by the gap between teaching and practice. No one should be surprised that some seek to close the gap by pretending that practice is other than it is or that defects in practice are very rare, that what appear to be defects are usually merely misunderstandings on the part of the uninformed. Those who take such a line seldom offer much convincing information. A great deal of honesty is necessary to clear the air. It is a scandalous violation of charity, justice, and even common sense to charge directly or by implication that those who speak out are unfaithful to the Church in some way or another.

THE PRIEST AND HIS SUPERIORS

Too often high ecclesiastical officials charge the outspoken with immaturity (this charge begins to appear as something of a pattern) or bad will or ignorance. Frequently in such cases it is possible, sometimes it is even quite simple, to devastate charges as made by a genuine appeal to facts and to right reason. Charges made against ecclesiastical authority are often ill-informed and irrational. They are sometimes prompted by emotion, sometimes by a desire for publicity. What is discouraging is that ecclesiastical authorities sometimes seem to disdain any attempt to reply as if the man might be a good and honest man, but ill-informed or demonstrably imprudent in judgment. The shrill cry of treachery too often seems to be the "matter of course" response. McKenzie was smart enough to write a book; articles are pounced upon much more quickly and intemperately. Furthermore, what he has to say appears well informed and carefully thought out. I hope many will read and think about what he has to say. A fresh mentality is not formed overnight; and a fresh mentality is what is needed in regard to matters of authority and obedience in the Church.

Priests are caught in the problem of authority more as subjects than as officials, but they are involved in the latter way. Few priests who are not senile are under the impression today that their authority will be taken seriously by the people if it seems to rest on a power structure. The faithful will obey their priest quite generally if they respect him as one who loves them and lives for them. There are still some situations in which a forceful priest can tyrannize over the faithful, but not many.

As subjects, priests are, more than others, victims of the abuse of authority, since those who have dominion over them have the means of making their lives very difficult indeed if they show any independence at all. Some priests have had recourse to the press, either directly or indirectly (through their followers), to defend themselves against their bishops and provincials. There is little doubt that many situations exist in which authorities are restrained by fear of publicity. Yet situations which appear monumentally unjust still occur.

The Code of Canon Law has come to be widely held in contempt, partly because it has been administered by bureaucrats who are ambitious and clever, capable of magnificently abstracting from the people involved in what to them is a "case."

Bishops, and even religious superiors, sometimes act toward their priests more like secular officials than like priestly brothers. The priest has little defense against the impersonal, bossy, "state your case in writing," type of bishop who treats him in a manner degrading to his human, let alone his priestly, dignity. He can be expected to pretend that he really believes the bishop's platitudes about brotherhood, concern, devotion to the Church, and so forth, which both know perfectly well as hypocrisy. Even basic civility, even the ordinary courtesies that would be found in secular life, can be denied. The Austrian report says: "The image of the priest as an ecclesiastical office-boy should change to that of an episcopal coadjutant."[8] This cannot be done unless priests have a genuine right to some participation in decision making. And it cannot be done overnight. Men who have lived much of their lives adjusting their minds to being "office-boys" are often incapable of becoming anything else.[9]

[8]*Cross Currents* (Summer, 1965), 272.
[9]In the encyclical on celibacy of Paul VI (June 24, 1967), the Pope says in par. 59 that the priest "will not be without the kindly care of his father in Christ, his bishop." This confusion of the real with the ideal, one of the elements of what has been called "triumphalism," fortunately is not unrelieved. Pars. 91-95 is an exhortation to the bishops to exercise human concern for their priests. The "fatherly" idea is barely acceptable if the bishop is sixty-five and the priest thirty, but it would all be more realistic and effective if a man-to-man relationship were stressed.

Church authorities have to remember that how things are done can have a decisive importance. The bishop must seek not only to save the priest's own sense of his worth, but he must make sure that his dignity is not destroyed in the minds of the people. How can anyone expect to attract modern young men, or even boys, to the priesthood, when the priests they know reach old age still being bossed about and hemmed in by rules more stringent than those the fathers they know lay down for their children?

A couple of points regarding the priest's exercise of authority over the laity: Since there is much less acceptance than formerly of the priest's authority by the laity, there is great danger of the priest restricting his activities to a tractable few. The priest must recognize that his priesthood is usually no longer enough to elicit respect, acceptance, obedience. He must possess the personal qualities to win for himself what formerly the office itself sufficed to gain.

> This change in the understanding of authority will make the priest's work more difficult. He can no longer content himself with the idea that ordination alone gives him all he needs to preach the Word of God convincingly and to represent to the laity an example of Christian living. The honor of the office will no longer hide personal inadequacies in the execution of the duties of office. Far higher claims are made of the priest today than in the past; if he cannot fill those claims, neither can he fall back on his authority, but at most only on the exterior tokens of respect attached to his office.[10]

RAHNER

Karl Rahner has a thoughtful article on obedience, chiefly religious obedience, which concerns mainly the religious priest and brother but has some relevance to the diocesan

[10]*Op. cit.*, Austrian report, 270.

priest as well.[11] I offer here some ideas drawn from these pages, without attempting to offer a digest of them.

Religious obedience is misunderstood; *mutatis mutandis,* so is the obedience of the diocesan priest. Obedience in religious life is not the obedience owed by children to parents. The purpose of parental authority is to render itself unnecessary. Many religious are childish, but since they should not be, the obedience owed by religious as such can hardly take its nature from these dwarfed beings. The superior makes himself ridiculous, imperils his authority, and renders obedience exceedingly difficult if he acts as if he were more wise, more prudent, more knowledgeable, and more devoted to the Church, to the apostolic mission of his order, and to its regular life than are his subjects. Obviously he is more one or the other than are some of his subjects, but that is accidental to the fact that he is superior. The superior should realize (and so should the subjects) that the faults of a man are more apparent when he is charged with higher obligations. Therefore humility is necessary to the superior and *charitable* tolerance must be exercised by the subjects.

Religious obedience is not *merely* for the sake of good order; it involves a profound commitment to a total way of life. But it is for the sake of good order; day-to-day obedience is just adult common sense. The superior should try to make obedience rational and pleasant by giving reasons for his commands, but subjects should not expect that everything, no matter how piddling, should be discussed. Subjects should be sufficiently mature to recognize that any life on this earth has its burdens, its minor irritations, and that the common life is no exception.

[11]*Mission and Grace* (London: Sheed and Ward, 1966), III, pp. 144-75.

"It is not true, even in religious communities, that all initiative should come from the superiors" (p. 152). The principle of subsidiarity has place in a religious community. Any human authority is limited in its influence on events. No superior should think that he initiates everything, and no subject should think that he is without responsibility for his actions. A superior is not merely to tolerate initiative on the part of his subjects; he should encourage it. A subject who refuses initiative is retreating from human obedience into subhuman subjection. Human authority must work with men and with conditions. A superior cannot command a man to do what that man is incapable of doing. He must "listen to," he must take into consideration the qualifications of the individual and the circumstances in order to effectively command. He must be obedient to the subject's potentialities and limitations, even if these limitations be deliberate on the part of the subject. "Be obedient to one another in Christ" (Eph. 5:21).

Religious obedience is not unlimited; it does not extend to all matters. Obviously we may not obey when a superior commands what is sinful. The unavoidable conclusion is that the subject must evaluate the command before he obeys. Yet Rahner notes that there are commands which are not morally evil but which are wrong (perhaps even culpably wrong on the part of the superior), but they must be obeyed. Why? Christ obeyed no man, but God alone. (Was he not disobedient to Joseph and Mary when their command was in no sense unreasonable? He departed the caravan and returned to Jerusalem, obviously against their will.) There is no clear "counsel" of obedience as there is of poverty and chastity. Rahner finds the only point to it the fact that "obedience is a permanent life-form giving man a God-ward orientation" (p. 163). But it is perfectly plain that obedience is to be given according to approved constitutions. (And for the diocesan priest, according to approved law, which is less easy to pinpoint.) With these limitations Rahner can say: "Whoever, therefore, is critical of the notion of religious obedience, is really attacking the wisdom of the life of the counsels in the Church" (p. 166).

Rahner ends with a strong point complementary to his point concerning the limitations of religious authority (". . . the superior can only command within the framework determined by the constitutions") and to McKenzie's point that the limitations of human authority imply that the subject must consider a command to know whether it is a valid one or not. Of course, both would recognize that often the common good and the public peace demand that commands which are not in themselves immoral be obeyed even though they exceed the commanding superior's authority. An issue can be too insignificant to warrant a contest. At the same time a subject must keep in mind that what may be insignificant to himself may be important enough in itself or to the community at large to require some action on his part. It can be an unreasonably heavy burden to place on one or two the need to curb an abuse of authority. That is precisely what happens when most accept such an abuse uncritically. Never must an honest attempt to clarify the limits of authority be looked upon as an attack on authority. It is precisely the opposite. Authority can be strong only when it remains within its limits.

Rahner's point is that religious obedience implies the risk of having to obey irrational commands as long as they are not immoral. He notes that, in any society, obedience to an unwise command is justified by the rational insight that such things are unavoidable in human society and are part of the original bargain. This is true in religious life as well; but in religious obedience there is the added factor that it is a conformity to the Cross of Christ who was "obedient unto death," a death decreed by a remarkably unwise and irrational command in the natural order but ultimately determined by God himself. If unwise commands were rendered invalid by their lack of wisdom ". . . obedience, which is always to some degree necessary, would end, for it would be left to the discretion of the subject to obey" (p. 169). At the same time Rahner insists that an act of obedience is a free act on the part of the one obeying. Therefore he is not exempt from the necessity of being morally certain that the act is a morally good one (*cf.* p. 171).

## MULLER

The best book on obedience in the Church that I know of is that of Alois Müller.[12] I have already referred to it. It offers a good survey of recent theological literature on the subject and an excellent and quite complete annotated bibliography. After a historical survey of Church authority from the New Testament to the present, the author considers the doctrine on Church authority and the moral theology of obedience. He then offers some well-thought-out reflections on authority and obedience in practice in the Church today. Though one will not always agree with the author, this book should be studied and reflected upon by those who hold authority, by those subject to authority, and especially by those who must form the young to a proper understanding of authority and obedience in the Church.

In noting some ideas based mainly on Müller's book, I wish to emphasize again, as I have in reference to the other authors I have cited, that I am not offering a capsule

---

[12]*Op. cit.* See footnote 5 above.

version of his book. I make no attempt to outline his entire position or even to represent his ideas exactly. I mention points he raises as they appear to me and with my reflections on them. I strongly recommend that you make use of what he has written.

To specify the current problem of obedience, Müller notes that most of what is written on obedience seems to be concerned with the necessity of obeying authority. Though he admits that disobedience is widespread, he calls this a chronic problem and not the specific problem of obedience which the Church faces now. The current problem confronts the obedient rather than the disobedient. He rejects as fallacious the argument that the superior's commands are more objective and reliable than the views of the subject, and he calls attention to the inconsistency of those theologians who accept the fact that all ecclesiastical pronouncements are not infallible yet in practice admit no room for dissent.

He defines what he considers the problem to be. It arises from widespread distrust of superiors who seem to wish to settle all disagreements by the simple *fiat* of authority. Often those who hold authority seem to be out of touch with real conditions and with the real reactions of both Catholics and non-Catholics. Müller holds, therefore, that, "the problem of obedience lies in the opposition between the will to obey and the objective good of the Church" (p. 134).

When there are signs that conditions are understood the distrust of authority melts away. Some would say that "true" obedience is not present when subjects desire evidence that the pattern of command is reasonable, but this is not the case. The Church is not running an army; the obedience it should seek implies the duty of normally giving right commands. The Church is probably governed as well today as it usually is, but that is not good enough in these times of the general decline of authority. A more sophisticated people rebel more sharply against injustice, against patronizing, domineering, close-minded authorities. The laity are expected to know their religion and to cooperate actively in the life of the Church. Such people will not be indifferent enough to take with "childlike trust" whatever authority has to offer.

Müller holds that, in the present situation, emphasis should be on the authority of God and of Christ rather than upon that of the institutional Church. The reaction to the Reformation was insistence on the hierarchical authority of the Church, upon its divine commission, to the extent that the impression is given that divine authority is delegated to the Church in such a way that it can function only through ecclesiastical authority. Now the brotherly nature of true Church authority should be clearly manifest, but this is hardly ever the case at all levels. The idea that in some cases the individual's rights must be sacrificed for the preservation of authority is disastrous in these days. Today the unforgivable mistake is for authority to refuse to admit mistakes.

Again we find in this author emphasis on the limitations of any human authority and the importance of open discussion. This last can be abused, as is the case with those who think that criticism is the only reaction of which man is capable. He says: "The Church of today needs vocal obedience, not silent disobedience; it needs an obedience that obeys to the limits, but that also speaks to the limits" (p. 134). He calls attention to the wise words of St. Thomas Aquinas concerning fraternal correction of one's own superiors (IIa, IIae, q. 33, a. 4).

He makes the important point that obedience is not the virtue which controls the intellect, that theology should not be "governed." Even when the magisterium rightly intervenes in theological discussion (which can happen before the necessity of rejecting heresy), it should normally be by way of theological argument rather than prohibition; theological argument can make prohibition superfluous, while prohibition without cogent argument may be without moral foundation. He does not refer to questions which have already been decided, but to matters however delicate which are still open questions.

If what I have said of Müller's positions make him appear intemperate, it does him injustice. He is scholarly, temperate, and applies conditions and qualifications with discrimination. His own words should be studied.

DOCTRINAL AUTHORITY

Since the question has just been raised, a few words are in order concerning the Church's doctrinal authority. This is not the place to treat the matter dogmatically, though there are many questions which need the consideration of dogmatic theologians. I wish only to point out a few problems which arise in the practical order as a result of what seems, especially in view of the temper of the times, to be an excessive desire on the part of ecclesiastical authority to "settle" matters which do not directly involve divine revelation.

Even the manuals of dogma generally make clear what is of divine faith and what is "theologically certain," and so forth. Unfortunately such distinctions were widely ignored for many years in seminary classes. Also unfortunately, what has been called "theologically certain" was not always quite so certain. Many priests have been badly shocked by some of the proposals of the "new theologians" who seem to be lightly rejecting the faith itself. I do not say that they never are; I would not even deny that some of them are rather irresponsible in their treatment of positions long held by most reputable theologians. It is true, however, that the shocks which many new approaches seem to cause are caused not by the approach itself but by the tenderness (or even ignorance) of the one shocked. When we see in the academic community how easy it is for a "recognized authority" in one field to pontificate in areas he knows little or nothing about, we should not be too surprised that men working in the neighborhood of infallibility sometimes slip into the habit of being infallible about some very fallible things. It should not be astonishing that an occasional cardinal seems to act as if he thought infallibility were contagious.

Universities have always been a problem and they always will be. The problem of academic freedom in the Catholic university may seem somewhat remote from the problems of the contemporary priest religious, but it is part of the whole problem of freedom and authority. Neil G. McCluskey, S.J., is quoted in the press as having said in a talk at the University of Dayton:

> . . . there is no more academic justification for the entry by a local bishop or provincial into the university discipline of theology than there is for the local mayor or governor to intrude into the field of political science. . . .
>
> Whatever the need that the bishop or provincial may have to exercise vigilance over the purity of Christian doctrine taught in secondary schools and parochial schools, the autonomy of the Catholic university precludes such treatment.

I suppose Father McCluskey has a special Bible which reads something about teaching the whole world except

Catholic universities which are quite able to teach themselves, thank you. Theology is a human science and as such is subject only to those versed in it, but it is a subalternate science which depends upon the "science of faith." The bishop is the teacher of the faith in his diocese. He can stick his nose into things he has no business with, but he is as much concerned with "the purity of Christian doctrine" in Catholic universities as he is anywhere else. To those who know something of academia it is laughable to place the "battle" of an American Catholic university with the local ordinary in the same context as that of the University of Paris with Stephen Tempier, Bishop of Paris. I suppose some "university people" are so good at "playing house" that if the name "university" were written on a barn the cows' milk would be called wisdom.

The problem again is the ridiculous assumption that any human freedom can be unlimited. With all the trouble Adam and Eve got into one would think their children would know better.

### THE BISHOP AND HIS PRIESTS

Archbishop Guilford Young wrote the introduction to the "Decree on the Ministry and Life of Priests" for *The Documents of Vatican II.*[13] He notes that the Decree provides clear doctrinal guidelines, but that it does not immediately solve the problem of freedom and obedience under which good priests labor today. He says that the priest is not the direct and immediate sign of Christ as the bishop is, but is rather an extension of the bishop, making the bishop present to the community. For this reason it is manifest that the priest must be loyal and obedient to the bishop. At the same time the Council calls for priests to be

[13](New York: Guild, America, Association, 1966).

mature human beings. "Bishops are exhorted to treat their priests as their helpers, counselors, brothers, and, indeed, friends" (p. 528).

Theory and practice are so far apart in this matter that for years a priest who referred to the discrepancy was figuratively tarred and feathered. He was insubordinate, impudent, a trouble maker, and was often publicly branded as "imprudent." Though this still is sometimes the case, a healthy change is taking place. Balanced and reputable priest scholars are calling attention to the need to bring practice into conformity with theory. I have already quoted Müller ("Ecclesiastical commands are hardly ever given in a brotherly spirit"), and Msgr. John Tracy Ellis says:

> It is possible that, if in the past the close personal relation-
> ships had obtained between bishops and priests that should
> characterize the relations of a father to his spiritual sons, more
> than one tragedy in the lives of the latter might have been
> averted. Nor is it too late to avert further tragedies that are
> now building up in the critical hour through which many
> American priests are passing.[14]

The decrees of the Council repeatedly call upon bishops to treat their priests as men, to have regard for their human and priestly dignity, to take them into their confidence, and to consult with them. It is not necessary to cite *Lumen Gentium, Christus Dominus, Presbyterorum Ordinis,* and so forth; they are well known and the excellent index to the edition of the Council documents already referred to will provide numerous exact citations. Here I wish to consider only one point.

Generally speaking the distinction between a senate of priests and an association of priests is clear. Theological-

[14]*Commonweal* (March 10, 1967), 648.

ly there is no problem whatsoever about the former. It is formed by the ordinary, presided over by him, and he holds veto power over its actions. In these days when the dignity and the consequent liberty of the human person is so constantly the concern of men of all classes and conditions, it is difficult to understand why such consultative bodies are not more commonly and more quickly established. Where and when they are established one would expect the bishop to constitute them as democratically as possible and to invest great confidence in them.[15]

An association of priests is another matter altogether. Such an association formed within a diocese, such as the Association of Chicago Priests, is constituted by the initiative of the priests themselves. Theologically it can be asked if there is any justification for such an organization. I believe that there is.

Such an association cannot be justified on the basis of any Council documents concerning priests as such. This is to be expected, since there seems to be nothing in the theology of the hierarchy and the priesthood which could justify such an organization. However, priests are men and they are Christians before they are priests. Ordination to the priesthood in no way suppresses their Christianity or their humanity. They freely waive the exercise of certain human rights to render themselves acceptable for ordination to the priesthood. Their promise of obedience to the bishop (or even the religious vow of obedience), however, does not enslave them. Both are made according to the rule of law and within limitations.

Any human authority, and that of the bishop is no exception, is quite capable of consciously or unconsciously

[15]*Cf. Christus Dominus,* par. 28.

overstepping its limitations. As human beings and as Christians, priests seem to have a perfect right, and perhaps even a duty, to join together to protect themselves against conscious encroachments on their human and Christian rights and to help the ordinary to avoid unconscious abuse of his authority. To continue the example already cited, the Cardinal Archbishop of Chicago has welcomed the help of the Association of Chicago Priests in this regard and has encouraged it to offer possible solutions to the problems of his great Archdiocese. In turn the membership has exercised temperance and wise restraint, "feeling out" as it were the establishment of guidelines for fruitful and devoted priestly cooperation with their bishop.

In these days of change and controversy a bishop who takes positions and exercises genuine leadership will find himself constantly opposed by some members of his flock. A wise bishop will welcome genuine dialog with his people and especially with his priests. In the nature of things dialog can be made to appear to be opposition by the irresponsible elements of the press, but thus far the relationship between the Archbishop of Chicago and the ACP has been a source of great edification to those who are not looking for trouble but are genuinely following what is going on. It is abundantly clear that the vast majority of the priests would drop the Association immediately if the organization appeared to challenge the rightful authority of the ordinary. The Archbishop's approval of and cooperation with the ACP has in fact enlisted the support of the vast majority of his priests in restraining the few extremists, most of whom will soon thank God for the steadying influence of their fellow priests.

The root problem is again the temptation to equate authority in the Church with worldly authority. The more one shares spiritual goods, the more one possesses them. With material goods the situation is quite the opposite. Obviously, then, authority in spiritual matters is quite different from authority in material matters.

CONGAR

In surveying the current literature on the subject of authority in the Church we can close by special attention to the wise and deep insights of Père Congar in his *Power and Poverty in the Church*.[16] He makes clear that, from the very beginning, the Church was an established community which could not be without authority, that the earliest Fathers insist on the notion of authority residing in the bishop. *"The insistence upon authority* has never been greater than in the writings of St. Ignatius of Antioch and of St. Cyprian" (p. 41). But authority is not so much *over* as *within* the Church. Cyprian notes that he always consults the lower clergy and seeks the approbation of the people, and we must remember that the clergy and the people elected their bishops. Everyone had a voice, since charismatic gifts could be found in the lowliest, but at the same time they were expected to flourish especially in the bishop who was chosen because he was a spiritual man.

Congar notes that the older parts of the ritual of consecration emphasize the duties rather than the powers of the bishop. The bishop's authority is to care for the welfare of the faithful, to serve the community. Gregory the Great observed to the Emperor's sister that St. Peter explained to the Church why he was baptizing Cornelius, and Congar wryly remarks how different is the spirit that prompted a high prelate of the Curia to say, "The characteristic proper to authority is that it does not have to give reasons."[17]

[16](Baltimore: Helicon, 1964).
[17]See *ibid.*, pp. 52-53, ft.

Moreover, through the fifth century great care was taken to keep the faithful informed of facts which today would be deliberately withheld from their knowledge.

Until well into the fifth century the clergy wore no special garb, nor was their rule of life markedly different from that of the faithful generally. This is an argument for doing away with special garb and special rules such as celibacy. However, no one denies that there are valid arguments on both sides of such questions. That such arguments exist does not mean that they are conclusive. This matter has been considered in the preceding chapter. The special garb and the other elements of the special way of life to a considerable extent are related more to celibacy than they are to ministerial office. Whether they are as necessary or useful now as they once were is, in my own mind, an open question.

Congar sees a great turning point in the notion of authority beginning with St. Gregory VII (1073-81). From this time on themes and texts originally applied to the Christian people begin to be applied to the pope alone.[18]

While Congar agrees with Hugo Rahner that the Ignatian (Loyola) notion of obeying God by obeying his representative is in continuity with the notion of authority first enunciated by St. Ignatius of Antioch, he adds that something new was introduced, namely, "a certain legalistic aspect" (p. 63). This important point is explained in this way:

> Legalism is characteristic of an ecclesiology unrelated to spiritual anthropology, and for which the word *ecclesia* indicates not so much the body of the faithful as the system,

[18]This development is well treated with extensive documentation by A. J. Carlyle in Vol. IV of the famous Carlyle, *A History of Mediaeval Political Theory in the West*, reprinted by Blackwood, London, in 1950.

the apparatus, the impersonal depositary of the system of rights whose representatives are the clergy or, as it is now called, the hierarchy, and ultimately the pope and the Roman Curia (p. 64).

The "spiritual movements" of the twelfth century, which in one form or another continued until the Reformation, and St. Bernard too kept insisting that more papal effort was devoted to preserving the tradition of Constantine than that of Peter.

(In passing we might note that Congar's essay on the ecclesiology of St. Thomas in his *The Mystery of the Church,* London, 1960, brings out the right thinking of Aquinas and the great contribution his thought can make to the questions of today. Unfortunately too many Thomists have tried to see in their master's teachings the ideas of the degenerate theology of their own times instead of reading him in historical context as Congar does.)

From the Council of Trent the besieged Church asserted and further centralized her authority on the one hand, and on the other some revision took place in the practice of authority. The strong assertion and the centralization resulted in authority becoming more remote and august, as it were; therefore ultimate and unchallengeable. This contributed to the revision, in practice, which might be described as a development of a "mystique" of authority wherein God's will is completely identified with institutional authority. The influence of the Society of Jesus had much to do with this. This has not been a bad thing, since at the same time much effort has gone into forming a diligent and holy clergy to exercise such authority. In point of fact, for well more than one hundred years at least, the popes and for the most part the bishops have given the world an example of responsible exercise of power and an authority of service.

Yet such authority is a temptation and has resulted in a formalism and depersonalization of relationships within the Church so that abstract justice and even "laws" are often served at the expense of persons; the "institution" takes precedence over people. Also the times have changed. The prefect order, discipline, and unquestioned obedience (or servility) of the Third Reich collapsed in miserable failure before a world which prided itself on being "free." Iron discipline can hardly win for the Church the respect of men today. The way of the blessed Christ can hardly be traveled in goose step.

It would be disastrous to think that there is no authority in the Church. Surely Jesus transformed the notion of authority (*cf.* Lk. 22:25), but as Congar says:

> It would be just as mistaken to think that the ideal of loving service eliminated all "power" as it would be dangerous to believe that authority in Christianity had reality or was defined *in the same way* as a juridical authority or a temporal power, with, as a kind of appendix, a moral obligation to exercise it in a spirit of service (p. 96).

He notes in conclusion that he does not suggest that the Church of charity and the Church of law are opposed, but that legalism has crept into appearances and practice. However, the Church today is quickly recovering from excessive claims to worldly forms of power. This passage deserves to be quoted.

> Can we as a rule enjoy privileges without coming to feel they are rights, or live in some degree of luxury without forming certain habits, be honored, flattered, treated with solemn and brilliant ceremonial, without setting ourselves morally on a pedestal? Can we always command and judge, receive men as petitioners, eager with their compliments, without getting into the habit of not really listening? In short, if we are always attended by thurifers, can we avoid acquiring a liking for incense? (p. 112)

Pope John did, and he affected the world as perhaps no other man of the twentieth century. His charming and winning personality made it quickly and abundantly clear that he did. So did Cardinal Meyer of Chicago, who seemed to have the personality of a bedpost, but whose humility penetrated the incense smoke like a fog beacon. Many prelates of our time continue to edify those who come in contact with them by their humility and by their genuine desire to give themselves in service to their people. All is far from lost and vast improvements are being quickly made, but the changes in the direction of simplicity that are being made and that will be made will greatly help to universalize the truly Christian spirit of authority so well exemplified by Pope John and by Cardinal Meyer.[19]

[19]See in addition to the material mentioned, *Obedience: The Greatest Freedom* (Boston: Daughters of St. Paul, 1966); and J. Ratzinger, "Free Expression and Obedience in the Church," in *The Church: Readings in Theology* (New York: P. J. Kenedy, 1963), pp. 194-217.

PART THREE:

# Seminaries and Seminarians

Charles J. D. Corcoran, O.P., M.A., Ph. Laur.

# 1: *Renewal in Seminary Life*

INTRODUCTION

The seminary does not have a fixed and immutable nature. It is a human invention which has taken different forms during its history and which can change further still. The form which it takes at a given time will follow the assumptions about human nature and about the priestly ministry held by those currently in authority. Vagarious is its history from the days of the Apostles who, it appears, used the apprenticeship method of training successors. Emperor Charles V was the first to apply the term seminary to this institution whose present format dates from the Council of Trent. That format is being seriously challenged at the present time.

Widespread experimentation with changes in seminary life has accompanied a reassessment of the assumptions underlying the seminary and its traditional policies. Experimentation, the application of known forms in new ways, has not sufficed. Exploratory efforts have been demanded, probing for new forms in answer to new situations and new insights of the Church in the modern world. Often this leaves the seminary director with some degree of anxiety and doubt. Even more does it bewilder the seminarian.

To stabilize and control the flow of change we must define the assumptions about human nature and the priesthood appropriate to our time and place in salvation history. We must examine whether silence and seclusion should be jettisoned along with celibacy and obedience, or whether modern psychology and other insights dictate the retention of these traditional elements of seminary life, albeit in altered form, *non nova sed noviter.*

The entire concept of seminary life in its presently-known forms is being challenged by something akin to the current death of God theology. We find a death of celibacy, a death of obedience, and a death of seminary-tradition movement that are espoused by laity, seminarian, and priest. Most vocal have been many ex-seminarians and ex-priests.

There is an element of reasonableness in any death of God theology, although it can easily be exaggerated and pushed too far. Judaism and Christianity were death of God theologies to the pagans who believed and worshiped differently. And we find in the death of celibacy and the death of obedience movements elements of reasonableness which must be included in our seminary *aggiornamento.*

The death of God theology emphasizes what God is not. Traditional philosophy and theology have always done this. God is not being; he is the cause of being. Being is only the creation of God. Cardinal Cajetan said: *Deus est super ens, super unum, super multum, etc.*

It is necessary from time to time to reflect on what God is not, to purify our notions of him. We must do this with our religious beliefs and practices and, indeed, with every aspect of our life, seminary life included.

The Holy See and Vatican Council II have led the way by saying what many religious practices are not. They are not up-to-date. They are not "aggiornamented." They must be made so, using as the criterion *avvicinamento,* oneness in Christ. Whatever is most closely united to Christ with the densest network of relationships is to be preferred. This is the principle of *avvicinamento,* which decides *aggiornamento* in each instance.

The Vatican Council told us what obedience is not in its doctrine of collegiality, what education is not in its suggestions for the reform of teaching, what celibacy is not when it urged a warmer life of brotherly and sisterly love within the convent as the form of chastity proper to religious life. Obedience is not sheepishness; education is not mere training; chastity is not the pure privation of embodied love.

When we clarify for the seminarian what so many things are not and aid him to understand what they really are, when we help him to a proper self-definition as a seminarian and a priest, we can validly expect that he will emerge from his present restlessness and doubt, turn to his vocation with total commitment, and attract others in increasing numbers to follow him. The general theory of the post-Tridentine seminary was explained by Cardinal Bourne:

> A seminary is not primarily a place of study. When the holy Council of Trent passed its famous decree for seminaries, the Fathers of the Council were not thinking principally of the need of study for the clergy, they were concerned chiefly about their sanctification. . . . The great founders—namely, Jean Jacques Olier and St. Vincent de Paul—had no thought of setting up new houses of study. . . . A seminary is a place the only essential object of which is to train to a truly spiritual and supernatural life. . . . There may be other ends and aims, but they must be wholly subsidiary to these. . . . It is true that since the sixteenth century seminaries have become more and more places of study. . . . But this important change is in no way incompatible with the primary and essential object of the seminary, provided it be not allowed to obliterate or even to obscure it. There is a real danger that it may be allowed to do so.[1]

The degree to which seminarians were secluded is indicated in the recommendations of Pope Leo XIII that major sem-

[1] Y. Allen, *A Seminary Survey* (New York: Harper and Row, 1960), pp. 373-74.

inaries be located in rural rather than urban areas in order to avoid worldly distractions. Pope St. Pius X wrote:

> Frequentation of the universities is not to be permitted to young clerics except for very grave reasons and with the greatest precautions on the part of the bishops. Seminarians must not be allowed to take part in secular polemics, and therefore We forbid them the reading of newspapers and periodicals, with the exception in a particular case of some periodicals of solid principle which the bishop may think useful for the student.[2]

## SPIRITUAL FORMATION

Spiritual formation within the seminary followed a pattern described as follows by the Maryknoll Spiritual Directory.

> The basic method used in ecclesiastical training houses to attain their purposes is the simple one of habit-forming practice: we learn by doing. Discipline, therefore, is imposed for only one reason: to enable the candidate to advance in acquiring as an habitual possession, a degree of that personal sanctification without which one may not properly enter the priesthood. . . . This training is chiefly an intensive repetition of certain acts inspired by supernatural motives—so that: (1) they are recognized by the individual as the correct acts in given circumstances . . . ; (2) they become easy to do when the circumstances arise in which they should be evoked; (3) they become almost automatic, second-nature or habitual, as a result of both conviction and practice.[3]

To some this smacks of programming an automaton for virtue, not the moral education of a free human personality. Even before Vatican II we find the Holy See pointing the way toward an improved moral pedagogy of those living in a seminary environment. Pope Pius XII was well aware of the inherent tendencies in boarding school life.

[2]Pope Pius X, *Pieni l'animo,* July 28, 1906.
[3]Allen, *op. cit.,* p. 378.

Doubtless, life in common, outside the natural environment of the home and under the direction of a strict rule which does not discern individual from individual does present its dangers. Regimentation, whether in studies, discipline, or prayer, tends to take away the sense of personal responsibility and degenerates into a mechanical act. Strict uniformity tends to suffocate personal impulse. Institutional life tends to hinder a broad vision of the world. And an inflexible imposition of regulations tends sometimes to foster hypocrisy or impose a spiritual level that for some will be too low and for others unreasonable. Too much severity ends in changing students of strong character into rebels, and the timid into dejected and introverted personalities.

These dangers can be remedied, Pius stated, by the three rules of discernment, moderation, and kindness. The ancient precept of "Virtue takes the middle path," should inspire the educator in every act, the Pope continued, whether in establishing a rule or in exacting its observance. He stressed that "the educator must see discretion in determining the amount of time for studies and for recreation, in meting out rewards or punishments, in granting liberties or imposing disciplinary measures." "Even religious exercises," he said, "require proper measures so that they do not become unbearable and tedious to the soul." A sense of duty, the Holy Father continued, should be inculcated through personal persuasion and affectionate reasoning. He warned that "there must not be a command without reasonable justification, a reprimand that carries personal rancor, or exclusively vindictive punishment."[4]

AUTHORITY IN THE SEMINARY

Being a person includes one's right to explore: to listen, not just to hear; to question, not just to understand; to choose, not just to consent. The one in authority has a duty to avoid being summary. Those under authority have an

[4]Pope Pius XII, allocution to the Students and Staff of the National Boys Boarding School of Rome, April 20, 1956.

obligation to shun indocility. There is a mutual duty to come to a meeting of mind and heart. Often that meeting will be at the level of reason. In the seminary it will be quite often at the level of faith. The seminarian may indeed have charismatic inspirations of the Holy Spirit, but those in ecclesiastical office have the authority of the final word, to be accepted in faith and docility. Authority does not render the subject supine; the subject does not render authority superfluous. Only in this way do all things work together unto good for those who love God.

It is unrealistic to expect the course of relationships between the seminarian and his superiors to run smoothly at all times. Emotional maturity does not come in a climate of perpetual sweetness and light. To a great extent it comes because adults take off their kid gloves and fight with youth. An adolescent's battles with his elders are as necessary as are his inner battles with himself.

Dr. Donald Holmes, a psychiatrist, has written that it is almost inconceivable that the average adolescent could carry off the stress of an intimate and protracted relationship with any adult without trouble arising between them, that a smooth and untroubled relationship is a reliable sign that they have managed to substitute an essentially unprogressive ceremonial sham for the authentic course of events.

Our culture (within the seminary and without) is suffering from an incomplete incarnation, largely from failure to integrate anger properly into our interpersonal relationships. Proper maturation and use of anger are indispensable to the work of fortitude, the hallmark of emotional maturity. Fortitude is the champion and defender of love and the virtues. Often, ideals are abandoned and aspirations unfulfilled not from failure to appreciate the desirability, but from lack of fortitude to champion the cause. This holds true in the

seminary as elsewhere. No adolescent can mature without
learning to use his anger. And for this he needs encounter
with the significant adults in his life.

Dr. Holmes says:

> Getting into arguments with the adolescent is both inevitable
> and useful. . . . It is the one medium of verbal communication
> in which a person of this age is likely to feel the most com-
> fortable. . . . When arguing, he is able to reveal things about
> himself which he could not possibly speak of in a quiet, exposi-
> tory tone. . . . If given the opportunity to rear up on his hind
> legs a little, he is able to confide much information about
> himself without experiencing the serious loss in self-esteem
> which would come of submitting helplessly to an omnipotent
> adult and pouring out his heart like a baby. . . . To argue
> back signals a measure of respect for the youngster's increasing
> capacity for self-determination.[5]

Argument is to be distinguished from bickering. In an
argument the issues are kept to the fore, so that the intellect
and will are engaged and the emotions recede, as the conversation advances toward the resolution of problems. Each
encounter should lead to a tentative resolution of differences and a closer approximation to mature collaboration
within the framework of authority and obedience.

"The celebrated rebellion of the adolescent," says Dr.
Holmes, "serves, at least in part, the purpose of attenuating
his dependence upon adults, and of reinforcing a more con-
fident sense of personal autonomy. This aim is roundly and
soundly defeated when his rebellion is sympathetically approved by the too-enlightened adult."[6] The adult must ally
himself with the youth's efforts to achieve a clearer and more
believable interpretation of reality, and against those forces
within him which wish to ignore or distort it. He does

[5]D. J. Holmes, *The Adolescent in Psychotherapy* (Boston: Little, Brown,
1964), p. 109.
[6]*Ibid.*, p. 10.

this by resisting the youth and insisting upon enforcement of certain reasonable standards of behavior, forcing the youth to be specific in his demands and in his criticisms. Feelings tend to be sustained by unanalyzed generalizations. The adult must press the youth to spell out precisely which individuals and which incidents have aroused his feelings. He must continue to ask: "Trust you with what, how much, how long, why, and under what conditions?" Only in this way does he help the youngster to bring his feelings before the forum of his own judgment and under the mastery of his own free will.

CONFIDENCE AND SELF-DEFINITION

The seminary years are the time of self-definition for the future priest, just as his later years will be the time of integrity, of fidelity to the self he has earlier defined. The seminarian must come to a judgment about himself which is not so much quantitative as qualitative: not, "How good am I?"; but "How am I good?" He does this, as Friedenberg has pointed out, by finding out what he is good at. It is the business of the seminary to help him make this discovery. He must be given opportunities to experiment, since the answer to his question can be discovered only by a series of approximations through trial and error.

There is more to life than finding the goal and seeing the path. There are the desire and hope of treading the path and reaching the goal. No one can remain long in love with something of which he has no hope. Together with the ideals of the priestly life the seminarian must be given confidence. The seminary must not only discover to the seminarian what he is good at; it must give him the feeling that he is good at it, the feeling of competence and adequacy, the conviction that what he aspires to is within his reach.

Here we come to one of the most delicate issues of seminary *aggiornamento*: the question of the confidence to be placed in the young students, the confidence they should be taught to have in themselves. Lack of confidence in, if not outright distrust of, the adolescent and young adult has flavored seminary directives. The diffidence extends not merely to the morals of young men but to their intelligence as well. Both are viewed as needing close custodial direction.

Concerning prospective candidates for the priesthood the Council of Toledo stated:

> Every age is prone to evil from adolescence onward; nothing is more uncertain than the life of an adolescent. This demands an arrangement whereby boys and adolescents destined for the clerical life reside in a common boarding place. To make sure that they spend these dangerous years of their lives not in sensuality but in ecclesiastical discipline, they should be under the guardianship of someone older and approved who will teach them discipline and oversee their lives.[7]

The same sentiments were echoed by the Council of Trent:

> The age of adolescence is inclined to pursue the pleasures of the world unless forestalled by proper training, and adolescents never would persevere in ecclesiastical discipline without an extraordinary grace from almighty God unless given a formation in piety and religious life from their tender years before opportunity for those vicious habits which tend to absorb men entirely.[8]

A like note of apprehension appears with regard to young priests. The *Directoire des grandes seminaires confies aux prêtres de la mission,* published in 1895 and reprinted in 1942, urges

[7]Mansi, X, cap. 24, 626.
[8]Mansi, XXXIII, sess. 23, *de. ref. can.* 18, 146.

. . . the advisability for young professors not to read a large number of authors in the field in which they are giving courses, since this is said to lead "only to a burdening of one's memory with a multitude of vague and incoherent ideas." Let them choose with the aid of the Superior and his most experienced associates four or five of the best authors who have investigated and clarified these questions.[9]

Speaking of young priests in the pastoral ministry, Pope Pius XII wrote in *Menti Nostrae*:

The passage from the sheltered and tranquil life of the seminary to the active ministry may be dangerous for the priest who enters the open field of the apostolate, if he has not been prudently prepared for the new life. You should realize that the many hopes placed in young priests may fail if they are not gradually introduced to the work, wisely watched, and paternally guided in the first steps of their ministry. We approve, therefore, the gathering of young priests when possible for some years in special institutions where, under the guidance of experienced superiors, they can develop their piety and perfect themselves in sacred studies and be put on the path toward that form of the ministry more closely corresponding to their temperaments and aptitudes. For this reason We would like to see institutions of this nature established in every diocese or, according to circumstances, for a number of dioceses together. In Our own Beloved City, We Ourselves did this when, on the fiftieth anniversary of Our priesthood, We erected the St. Eugene Institute for young priests.[10]

How warranted is this paternal solicitude? How much confidence can we place in aspirants to the priesthood and the freshly ordained priest apart from the cautious safeguards mentioned above? Freud himself was no romantic optimist about human nature. Arthur O. Lovejoy says that one need not believe in Original Sin to be convinced that there is something radically wrong in human nature. One need only consult the history or the present behavior of

[9]Allen, *op. cit.*, pp. 379-80.
[10]Pope Pius XII, *Menti Nostrae*, September 23, 1950.

# Renewal in Seminary Life

the human race. He cites numerous authors down the centuries to the same effect. Is there something about human nature and the requirements of the priesthood which demands that the younger live in close apprenticeship to the elder until a priestly career is well launched? It would seem so, though the form may differ with time and place. The British psychologist, Alexander Shand, helpfully describes the emotional stages which are passed by the youngster on his way to becoming what St. Paul called "a law unto himself," mature enough to be left in the hands of his own counsel.

> The result of the modification which the systems of the emotions undergo in man, and especially the multiplication of the causes which excite and sustain them, is (1) to make man the most emotional of animals, and (2) to render possible the debasement of his character. For that which is a condition of his progress is also a condition of his decline—the acquired power of ideas over emotions, and the subsequent power of each indefinitely to sustain the other. Hence the existence of the emotions constitutes a serious danger for him, though not for the animals, and the balance which is lost when the emotions are no longer exclusively under the control of those causes which originally excite them can only be replaced by the higher control of the sentiments. There are then three stages in the evolution of emotional systems: the first and primitive, in which they are under the control of the stimuli innately connected with their excitement, undergoing a certain change through individual experience, but not radically altered; the second, in which they become dangerous and independent systems; the third, in which they are organized under the control of the new systems which they are instrumental in developing. For it is with them as so often with children, who at first have to obey a rule imposed on them which they cannot understand, and afterwards, when they grow up, break from its control, but only to fall under their own unregulated impulses, until, at length, their disasters teach them to make a new law to replace the old one they derided.[11]

11A. F. Shand, *The Foundations of Character* (London: Macmillan, 1914), pp. 195-96.

STAGES OF MATURITY

Progress to personal maturity moves through three periods: from dependence, through dependability, to independence. The critical years are the intermediate ones, in which dependability is established. These are the seminary years, and they are years marked by a growing sense of responsibility. They see the maturation of the human reasoning power, accompanied by a last great step in the assimilation of the realities of life. Authorities have marked off three main cycles in the growth of the human mind, running to a span of seven years each. A newborn baby has a blank and undeveloped mind. During his first seven years a child develops the ability to understand things when they are explained to him. Because this capacity is sufficiently advanced by the age of seven, a child is sent to school where things are explained to him methodically. During the second cycle of seven years the youngster develops the ability to figure things out for himself; not everything equally, but primarily those things which have personal reference. If this ability is properly cultivated, a youngster should enter adolescence with firm convictions about himself and his ultimate destiny. During the third and final cycle of seven years a youth develops the ability to figure out for himself matters which relate to society and to the world at large. And so, about the age of twenty-one a youth is emancipated politically and economically, empowered to vote and qualified to enter validly binding contracts.

Wise seminary directors will recognize this natural unfolding of youthful mental powers by drawing the seminarians more and more into serious discussion about the larger problems of life, encouraging their participation in the works of mercy or apprenticeship to their future ministry. This will supply a healthy social counterpoise to the previous exaggerated emphasis on the purely individualistic aspects of spiritual formation in the life of the seminarian.

Superiors, in practicing "togetherness," should draw the seminarians, as far as their maturity permits, into adult activities, priestly activities. If "togetherness" means only that the elders share the play and recreation of the younger members of the community, the latter will make the former childish instead of the elders making the younger more mature, more seasoned in virtue.

Adolescence is a phenomenon unique to civilization. In very primitive societies there is no such thing as adolescence, because the life of an adult is so rudimentary that no period of apprenticeship or special preparation is needed. The more civilized a culture becomes, the more does society tend to lengthen the time of adolescence. At the early end the privileges of adolescence are anticipated by children too juvenile to use those privileges responsibly. At the latter end the responsibilities of adulthood are postponed, often with ruinous and irreversible consequences. Prolonged schooling during which the youth is treated more like a child than an adult is one of many contributing factors, and a principal one in the case of the seminarian.

Adolescence is an awkward age of partial dependence and incomplete independence. The seminarian is caught in the tension of a four-way stretch: between his longing for independence and his need of a refuge to which he can fly as a dependent when he finds himself overmatched by the problems of life; between his elders' desire to see him independent and their wish to have him depend upon their experience and better judgment. It can be a very trying time for the youth and for the adults in his life. Dr. Holmes comments that dealing with adolescents is "an experience which constantly reminds one that there are many easier forms of livelihood."

The best qualities of adolescents are brought out primarily in the company of those of their own sex and of nearly their own age. Such companionship should constitute the steady diet of social life. The company of the opposite sex and of adults should be blended in, but with a frequency and degree which allow of a smooth transition to heterosexual relationships and adult status.

In daily life a human being is presented with countless opportunities for the practice of temperance: in eating and dressing, in speech and deportment. Relatively rarer are the obvious occasions for exercising fortitude, the champion and defender of temperance. As a nation's standard of living is elevated, the miseries of life are eased and the demands for practicing fortitude diminish further. The modern cult of "tender, loving care" and our cultural avoidance of anger can act counter to the demands of fortitude in the moral development of the seminarian. Christ knew how to be vigorous as well as tender with his seminarians, the Apostles; he could show anger toward them and elicit their anger and their protest. This is required to help another to manhood.

The transition from play to work is central to the process of growing up. Play makes an important contribution to one's maturity. Play is joyful. No one can live the sorrowful mysteries of life successfully unless he knows how to live the joyful. The Bible associates play with wisdom. Play in this sense is work which has made the transition from earlier forms of play with complete success. Play, then, is the consummate performance of which a human being is capable in any field of work, as when a master speaker plays on the emotions of his audience, or when a master musician plays on the keyboard of a musical instrument. It is in this sense that wisdom ran playing before God as he made the world. This ease of performance which accompanies wisdom, affectionate thinking, this play will show itself in a suppleness of mind and body, of thought and emotion, in the life of the seminarian and in the example of his directors.

The immature tend to ask: "Is it easy and is it pleasant?" The mature ask: "Is it worthy and is it possible?" Responsibility consists in doing what is worthy and possible, regardless of whether it is easy or pleasant. Here, again, our modern cult of feeling can be a handicap. God has built great durability into human nature. If you walk in your shoes, the soles wear thin. But, if you walk in your bare feet, the soles grow thicker. True, you can create a sore by picking at healthy flesh, if you are irritated when you should be stimulated. But, if activities and tasks are carefully graduated in degree of responsibility and difficulty, the youngster's durability and competence will develop symetrically with the increasing demands of his life.

It is generally agreed that a growing youngster cannot be seriously harmed developmentally if, when he is ready to move into a new area of growth, he is not prevented from doing so and is not deprived of the means necessary. But the growth of youngsters can seem a threat to their elders. The seminarian requires teachers and directors who can tolerate maturity in those under their care.

Maturity is an analogous concept. Each time we speak of it we have a somewhat different meaning in mind. The maturity of an apple is different from that of a rose. The flower is maturity for the rose bush. The flower, the apple blossom, is merely a forerunner of maturity in an apple tree. The maturity of a woman is not the maturity of a man. The maturity of the extrovert is not the maturity of an introvert. This analogousness extends even to the level of individual differences. Each human being's maturity will show unique characteristics, encouraged and fostered by God as part of his doctrine of personal immortality. In the perfect maturity of eternal life in heaven each human being is unique in his maturity.

The question of maturity in a seminarian cannot be divorced from the question of his superior's maturity. Modern psychology does not trust the measurement of a pupil without some measurement of the teacher, for in the hands of a different teacher the pupil will measure differently. To the query "How well does this violin play?" we must respond by asking, "Who is playing it?" Even a Stradivarius sounds different when played by a virtuoso and then by someone else. Some superiors do not tolerate mature behavior in their subjects. They fail to draw a proper distinction between childlike and childish, sheeplike and sheepish. As pastors they insist on sheepishness in their sheep; as superiors they demand childishness in their subjects, and persist in treating seminarians and young priests far below the dignity and maturity demanded by their years.

### Authority and Obedience

Vatican II took a major step toward revitalizing the authority-obedience relationship when it extolled the charismatic gifts and services by which the faithful collaborate actively with the hierarchy. Supine obedience, wherein the subject is the marionette of the superior, is simply not a Christian concept. It has no place in the seminary.

Authority is bound up with authorship. Primarily, authority is the attribute of the author, of the one who originates and gives growth, of the one who begets and cherishes. Authority belongs first of all to God the Father, from whom proceed the Son and the Holy Spirit. Our Divine Lord taught us this authority when he said of himself: "I came down from heaven not to do my own will, but the will of him who sent me" (Jn. 6:38). He repeated the lesson at the Last Supper when he said of the Holy Spirit: "He shall not speak of himself; but what things soever he shall hear, he shall speak" (Jn. 16:13). St. Paul underscores the same divine authority when he says: "Therefore, neither he that planteth is anything, nor he that watereth; but God that giveth the increase" (1 Cor. 3:7). God is the author of all things, and the source of all authority. Others hold their capacity for authorship, and their authority, only from him.

The ability to relate his authority to the fatherhood of God will be a great help to the seminary director seeking to administer his office with loving wisdom and affectionate influence. And, conversely to this, the ability to relate obedience and vocation to the divine missions and processions will aid the seminarian who must live under authority. The noblest motivation and the richest growth in wisdom and grace will come to those who order their lives in the light of these relationships.

In a very illuminating chapter on the nature of authority, Father Thomas Gilby, O.P., warns of the constant danger that this notion of authorship, of living fruitfulness, as the essence of authority, may be lost in the mechanics of executing authority at the human level.

> The very efficiency of institutional discipline produces a special danger, that of substituting a pattern laid on for a quickening impulse from within. . . . Authority hardens into legal office, about which the claim to jurisdiction sometimes seems more prominent than the blessing conferred. . . . And the effect is that of business organization rather than of companionship, the emphasis falls on correctitude rather than virtue, the atmosphere is one of strain rather than of ease, and the first words heard by those who approach it from without are a demand for their submission, not an invitation for their com-

pany. All this is overstated, but that is commonly the way with dangers.

The meaning of authority has hardened. So also the meaning of the related concepts of prince and lord, perhaps partly owing to the influence of language and the translation of terms from Greek to Latin. Where the Greeks saw the movement of things, the Romans insisted on their proper position; between the Politics and the Roman Law is the difference between *orexis* and *gravitas,* between purpose and place, between desire and due. St. Benedict keeps the old sense when he reminds abbots, *majus est prodesse quam praeesse*; but on the whole the old naturalness and ease were lost in the growth of civil and ecclesiastical organization. Prince came to mean less an originator than a dignitary, and lord less a ratifier or validator than a magnate. Later government, says Sir Ernest Barker, "became a matter of *principatus,* of the 'first place' or pre-eminence, rather than of initiative."[12]

Authority can exist at one of three levels, depending upon the maturity of the governed and the governing: at the level of might, of right, or of sight. Superiors, especially parents, impose their authority upon subjects too immature to understand their elders' right or to have the sight to see for themselves what ought to be done. But, as Gilby points out, "one day parents find that they have to explain themselves to their children." As youngsters develop the ability to comprehend such explanations, superiors have an obligation to respect their growth and add appropriate explanations when they impose their authority. In this way the youngster will mature to the point where authority will be operative by reason of sight, as the maturing young man sees for himself what should be done and anticipates the will of his superiors, manifesting what has been called active or creative obedience.

You will notice a parallel relationship between these three stages of authority (as might, right, and sight) and

[12]T. Gilby, *Between Community and Society* (London: Longmans, 1953), pp. 309-10.

the three principal acts of prudence: counsel, decision, and decisive action. Prudence, like any other habit, can be acquired only by a person who is allowed to practice it. In the early stage the seminarian may not share in counsel or decision, but he should be allowed some leeway in the last prudential step, that of decisive action. Something of the seminarian, and not merely of his superiors, should be reflected in his performance.

In the second stage, of authority by right, the seminarian begins to enter in a real though subordinate way into the decision about what is to be done, the decision about time, place, and other circumstances surrounding what is to be done. Apprenticed to the prudence of his elders in this way, as a subordinate but respected practitioner, he will slowly acquire the ability to form his own counsel and to help others in forming theirs.

Thus seminary directors will send their charges forth into the ministry, having fulfilled their own part in the divine work mentioned by Ecclesiasticus: "God made man from the beginning, and left him in the hands of his own counsel. He added his commandments and precepts. If thou wilt keep the commandments and perform acceptable fidelity forever, they shall preserve thee" (Ecclus. 15:14). This simple scriptural statement of educational policy and of human dignity will enable the seminary director to quickly regain his bearings when he feels lost in the complexities of spiritual formation.

# 2: The Spiritual Formation of the Seminarian

The Church is presently seeking increased openness in two directions: in the direction of the roots of the Christian life in the Bible, the early Church and the saintly founders of religious traditions; in the direction of the fruits of the Christian life and the world which must bear those fruits. The renewal of seminary formation must include both forms of openness, giving primary emphasis to the roots of the Christian and priestly life.

## Human Nature and Human Destiny

It would be useless to discuss openness if man's nature were closed and determined. Contemporary theologians, therefore, emphasize the openness of human nature. Man, they say, is a project to himself. God leaves human nature somewhat undetermined. He offers human nature to each individual as a set of possibilities which the recipient must fashion for himself in his own unique way. Man must project himself into the future from the roots to the fruits intended for him by God's personal providence.

Using the transcendental *a priori* method to supplement the traditional *a posteriori* method, theologians search out the presuppositions of human nature and human destiny as found in Christ and in each Christian. Transcendental anthropology is the name given to this study of man. Karl Rahner writes:

> The question of man and its answer . . . must be looked upon as the soul of dogmatic theology. . . . We can develop

a Christology today only from the standpoint of such a transcendental anthropology. . . . A Christology which is developed
merely *a posteriori* cannot be integrated into a comprehensive
evolutionary understanding of the world and cannot escape the
suspicion of being mythology.[1]

Father Rahner claims that by the use of this approach
he is introducing into theology insights which never before
appeared. We must be open to such possibilities, especially
during these days of experimentation when the Church itself has opened its mind to a renewed vision of things.

It is premature to present anything like a final judgment or a finished picture on any matter now under experimentation in the Church. Only experimentation will
decide the validity of applying the transcendental method
to the daily examen, to meditation, to the problems of
seminary formation. Presently we can at best, like Father
Rahner, offer suggested directions of thought which may
enter the final synthesis. The present chapter, therefore, is
not intended to have the inner unity of a finished synthesis,
but the extrinsic unity of various suggestive thoughts relating to one subject, the spiritual formation of the seminarian.

In discussing the roots of seminary formation some
have felt that the tradition of spiritual theology followed
in the formation of seminarians has not been ecclesial
enough, that it tends to be irrelevant to and somewhat
aberrant from the common spiritual life of the people of
God. Westow claims that the modern liturgical revival in
the Church did not arise from the tradition of spiritual
theology found in the seminaries.

Westow traces this latter tradition to its origins in the
Middle Ages. He writes:

---

[1] Karl Rahner, S.J., "Theology and Anthropology," in T. P. Burke, *The
Word in History* (New York: © Sheed and Ward, Inc., 1966), pp. 1-2.

In the religious literature of the Middle Ages the sense of community grew weaker and weaker. The whole accent of progress between, roughly, the eleventh and the sixteenth centuries falls on the first person singular. . . . And the spiritual life abounds in highly individual forms of spirituality, visions, revelations, and somewhat peculiar expressions of mystical experience. . . . Already in St. Bernard we find that the language is emotional, individual, and erotic. But whereas St. Bernard still sways in his sermons from the Church as the Bride of Christ to the individual soul, in the exercises of St. Gertrude the Church is not mentioned. From there the tradition developed. . . .

Now, insofar as these developments brought about a great refinement of mind and heart; developed the beginnings of a true dogmatic, moral, and mystical theology; inaugurated the discoveries of psychology; in short, showed forth the almost indefinite facets of the human person as an individual, this period in our history made a lasting contribution which was both sound and necessary. But insofar as it led to an over-concentration on the individual; taught men to analyze without end; overstressed the importance of purely individual experiences and emotions; and brought about an individual sensitiveness and complication which might easily upset the delicate balance of society, it could have disastrous effects.[2]

PERSONAL FORMATION

Every human emphasis carries within it the danger of overemphasis, which ends by downgrading or neglecting things deserving of proportional emphasis. We have seen some of those dangers come to realization in the past history of the seminary. We must be on the lookout for them today. There is a danger inherent in "personalism," for example, that the individual will take everything personally, so that correction and direction are no longer accepted with any sort of objectivity. If pride and one-up-man-ship are not checked, there is danger that the currently voguish "I-Thou" relationship will be defeated because

2T. L. Westow, *The Variety of Catholic Attitudes* (New York: Herder and Herder, 1963), pp. 46 ff.

each "I" thinks he is "It." New terminology will not suffice, a change of the name without a change of the game. The new terms still leave the ancient human need for mortification of egoism and egotism. No amount of optimism about the human person can hide the inclinations to sin which remain within a person after Baptism. No amount of environmental manipulation or of interpersonal relationships can dispense with the need to discipline those intrapersonal inclinations, to master them by penance and mortification.

It is the work of wisdom to "see life steadily and see it whole." We must be sure that we include all the essentials in our plan of seminary formation and that we emphasize each essential in a way which contributes to the proper emphasis of each and every other essential. The values of life are interdependent. The growth of each requires the development of every other. Emphasis upon personal development increases the need of community life. Liturgical and community life, in turn, can grow only with the deepened personal formation of each participant. Freedom is not enhanced by the refusal of obedience. The subjective dignity of the person is not furthered by the denial of objective norms of conduct. Only by the acceptance and development of all the essentials will the seminarian conform himself to the image of Christ the Priest.

We might say that the seminary has suffered from the malady of incomplete incarnation. It is not unique in this. Rather, it shares a problem common in modern life. Herzberg might well have been speaking of the seminary when he said: "Industry, as the dominating institution in our society, must recognize that if it is to use human beings effectively, it must treat them in terms of their complete nature rather than in terms of those characteristics that appear to be suitable to their organization."[3] The seminary must avoid producing model seminarians rather than young priests whose growth potential has been maximized by a seminary formation kept constantly relevant to the times in which we live. An obvious observation, indeed, but one necessary to make because we are dealing not with a tendency which can be eliminated from the seminary once and for all, but with a tendency which will reinstate itself in any organization when vigilance is relaxed: the tendency to produce organization men rather than men oriented primarily toward their mission in life. Overlooking the obvious, neglecting the ordinary, is a greater threat to success in life than failure to take account of the extraordinary. It is a master of inattention, not lack of intelligence or good will. Seminary authorities will not eschew any proposal which makes for a fuller incarnation, which will help decrease dissatisfaction and increase satisfaction with seminary life.

It may come as a surprise to learn that these latter two purposes are not the obverse and converse of each other. Removing dissatisfaction in seminary life will not increase the satisfaction; nor will an increase in satisfaction bring a decrease in dissatisfaction.

A STRUCTURED LIFE

Herzberg distinguishes two sets of human needs: hygiene needs, concerned with the avoidance of dissatisfaction, and related to mental illness; and motivator needs, concerned with satisfaction and related to mental health. The factors underlying the two sets of needs are not polar opposites of the one continuum. They constitute two different con-

[3]F. Herzberg, *Work and the Nature of Man* (New York: World, 1966), p. 170.

tinua. Factors relating to motivator needs (achievement, recognition, work itself, responsibility and advancement) contribute very little to dissatisfaction. Dissatisfying factors (such as company policy and administration, supervision, interpersonal relations and working conditions) contribute very little to job satisfaction.

Failure of industry to deal with human nature holistically is ascribed by Herzberg to its exaggeration of hygiene needs and its neglect of motivator needs. The seminary can profit from the lessons learned in other human enterprises when it implements the changes demanded by *aggiornamento*. To this end it is necessary to have a full confrontation between the proponents of personalism and those who counter them in the name of system and order, between the champions of the seminarian's hygiene needs and the champions of his motivator needs.

A structured and scheduled life in the seminary apprentices the future priest to a reality which he must later create in his own life. To the extent that he is still an apprentice (the earlier seminary years), the student must have the structure imposed. To the extent that he has served his apprenticeship (the latter seminary years), the student should collaborate in determining his own schedule.

Psychiatry has found that where authorities impose no definite structure on the life of their charges youngsters begin pathologically to impose structure or punishment upon themselves. And the pathological imposition is invariably more rigid and repressive than the obligation which was shirked. The healthy struggle which should occur between the youngster and authority is avoided, but it does not vanish. It is internalized in the form of neurotic conflict, and externalized in the form of neurotic relationship to the environment.

213

# Seminaries and Seminarians

Seminary authorities, therefore, must be sensible but vigorous champions of discipline and order in the life of the young student for the priesthood. The healthy use of anger, in imitation of Christ, is an essential element of Christian incarnation for the seminarian and his director. The seminarian who does not have his rebellious anger disciplined by confrontation with the mature anger of his elders will emerge from his training with an incomplete incarnation of the Christian life. The seminary director who can never get angry is lacking an incarnate essential of his office. He must, however, constantly point out that he is emulating the example of Christ in his anger, so that his behavior is seen by the seminarian as a supernaturally motivated act.

Speaking to this point, Vatican Council II said:

> Let discipline be exercised, then, in a way which will develop in the students an internal attitude by which the authority of superiors will be accepted through an act of personal conviction, that is, conscientiously (cf. Rom. 13:5) and for supernatural reasons. The rules of discipline should be applied in accord with the age of the students so that they can gradually learn to govern themselves, to make wise use of their freedom, to act on their own initiative and energetically, and know how to work along with their confreres and lay people as well. The whole seminary program, permeated with a cultivation of reverence and silence and with a concern for mutual help, should be structured as a kind of introduction into the life which the seminarian will lead as a priest.[4]

The Council recommends the cultivation of silence. Contemporary psychology has something interesting to contribute here. Experiments in sensory and perceptual depriva-

[4]Excerpts from the Decree on Priestly Formation are taken from *The Documents of Vatican II*, published by Guild Press, Association Press, America Press, and Herder and Herder, and copyrighted 1966 by The America Press. Used by permission.

tion indicate that humans require a certain quantity, variety, and orderliness of sensory input. When input falls below need in these respects, the mind is thrown back upon its own resources and one of two things tends to happen. If the mind has been properly prepared by previous experience and discipline, there will be a period of growth and creativity. If the mind is immature, abnormal or unprepared by previous experience, there will be a period of cognitive and emotional disintegration, accompanied sometimes by hallucinations and severe anxieties.

Einstein wrote: "I lived in solitude in the country and noticed how the monotony of a quiet life stimulates the creative mind." Rokeach adds: "We know from recent work on sensory deprivation that solitude and monotony can stimulate all minds, creative or not."[5]

The great holy men of every culture and era have found sensory deprivation a necessary condition of inner growth. It is also a uniquely helpful means of self-revelation. One's true self is revealed best under stress, especially the stress of privation. Some degree of solitude and sensory deprivation will have to be retained in seminary life, then, for the double purpose: of testing a seminarian's present development, and of stimulating further growth. A necessary concomitant, direction by one versed in the discernment of spirits (or, as we would say today, the psychology of Christian development) will also remain an abiding feature of seminary years.

Benefit is derived from sensory deprivation only where there has been proper input. The seminarian cannot be cut off from contact with the sources drawn upon by the mature leaders and scholars of his generation. Modern methods of

[5]G. A. Stwiner, *The Creative Organization* (Chicago: University of Chicago Press, 1962), p. 67.

communication and transportation make it feasible to combine the advantages of both worlds: the world which supplies input and the world which provides needed solitude and deprivation. Arrangements of this sort have been discussed in meetings of combined seminary faculties, and experiments in this direction have been undertaken in some instances. The same point of view is carried over into programs of apprenticeship in the pastoral ministry. A balance is struck between personal growth and communication with others, whether to learn from them or to help them. It is the process of feedback implied in the ancient mendicant motto: *comtemplata aliis tradere*.

We find the essential wisdom of traditional seminary practice vindicated in the remarks of Berger and Luckmann, contemporary social scientists.

> To have a conversion experience is nothing much. The real thing is to be able to keep on taking it seriously; to retain a sense of its plausibility. This is where the religious community comes in. It provides the indispensable plausibility structure for the new reality. . . . Religion requires a religious community, and to live in a religious world requires affiliation with that community. The plausibility structures of religious conversion have been imitated by secular agencies of alternation. The best examples are in the areas of political indoctrination and psychotherapy.
>
> The plausibility structure must become the individual's world, displacing all other worlds, especially the world the individual "inhabited" before his alternation. This requires segregation of the individual from the "inhabitants" of other worlds, especially his "cohabitants" in the world he has left behind. Ideally this will be physical segregation. If that is not possible for whatever reasons, the segregation is posited by definition; that is, by a definition of those others that nihilates them. The alternating individual disaffiliates himself from his previous world and the plausibility structure that sustained it, bodily if possible, mentally if not. In either case he is no longer "yoked together with unbelievers," and thus is protected from their potential reality-disrupting influence.

Such segregation is particularly important in the early stages of alternation (the "novitiate" phase). Once the new reality has congealed, circumspect relations with outsiders may again be entered into, although those outsiders who used to be biographically significant are still the dangerous ones. They are the ones who will say, "Come off it, Saul," and there may be times when the old reality they invoke takes the form of temptation.

Alternation thus involves a reorganization of the conversational apparatus. The partners in significant conversation change. And in conversation with the new significant others subjective reality is transformed. It is maintained by continuing conversation with them, or within the community they represent. Put simply, this means that one must now be careful with whom one talks (Berger, P. and Luckmann, T.: *The Social Construction of Reality*. N.Y.: Doubleday, 1966, pp. 145-46).

A similar combination of input and privation is the way to emotional growth and maturity. It is fully compatible with a life of celibacy. If a neurotic, sick in his power to love and to dare, can be restored to health by psychiatric procedures which involve no trespass of celibacy, then a normal person can grow in love and courage in the celibate life. Non-celibate communication is not at all an indispensable prerequisite of personal growth and emotional maturity.

Seminarians must have the opportunity of a sufficient range of emotional relationships to stimulate constant healthy development. Just what form those relationships will take is a matter to be worked out in collaboration with family and friends. Certainly there is no ready-made pattern to be accepted from the world, whose restless pursuit of emotional stimulation demonstrates that it has not solved the problem for itself.

The life of the seminarian spans late adolescence and early adulthood, when the young man learns to completely fulfill on his own initiative the responsibilities flowing from a self-definition which includes his relationships to the world within, the world around, and the world above. The seminarian learns "to accept in all circumstances the verdict and the demands of charity in all their details." These are the words of Dom Ryelandt, who goes on to describe the method of spiritual formation utilized by Christ and Church.

> Christ is the master who by the gift of the Holy Spirit works on the sub-conscious . . . to enkindle in it the need of truth and of intimate union, and to develop an intense desire to seek out God and his holy will. . . . The Church is for us just what Jesus was: the way, the truth and the life. . . . Just as the apostles said to the Savior: 'Lord, teach us to pray,' so we must turn to the Church. . . . Now our Lord did not give the disciples a reasoned psychological system: he recited the Pater; and it was a direct lesson example.
>
> The Church adopts the same method. . . . She forms her children not by any methodical, reasoned system but by the repetition of her own prayer. In the liturgy of the missal and the breviary she prays before us, she prays for us and with us. . . . By this communion of life she completes in us in Christ and through the Holy Spirit the grace of divine adoption.
>
> [Still] because the lessons we receive from the liturgy through its epistles, gospels, etc., are not systematic, and as our mind needs a certain order to enable it to comprehend truths, even religious truths, it must be given a serious intellectual formation corresponding to the individual needs concurrently with the liturgical instructions, a rational exposition of the faith, positive dogmatic theology.[6]

The thought of Dom Ryelandt is in faithful harmony with that of Vatican Council II in its *Decree on Priestly Formation*. That thought offers a sane and balanced compromise in the current dispute between the advocates of personalism and the advocates of system in the formation of seminarians. The conciliar Decree states:

[6]Dom I. Ryelandt, O.S.B., *Union with Christ* (Dublin: Clonmore and Reynolds, 1966), p. 67.

Spiritual formation should be closely linked with doctrinal and pastoral training. Especially with the help of the spiritual director, such formation should help seminarians learn to live in familiar and constant companionship with the Father, through Jesus Christ his Son, in the Holy Spirit.[7]

## EDUCATIONAL NEEDS

If the seminarian needs theology to fully profit from the liturgy, he needs philosophy for the full benefits of theology. And if his education in theology should be systematic, so also should his philosophical training be. Certain authors urge the advisability of teaching philosophy and theology concurrently in the seminary, for the optimum spiritual formation of the seminarian himself and as the best preparation for the priestly role. Other experienced seminary teachers reject the wisdom of such a plan. Here, again, we face an issue which must be decided by prudent experimentation.

Father Robert Johann, S.J., has explained the helpfulness of philosophy for the seminarian who is deciding and developing his vocation in life.

> Philosophy (as an exploration of the experiential situation in which the Word is supposed to take root) has something of its own to contribute in forming the priest, unattainable in any other manner. (It assists him) to develop that habit of reflection whose horizons are wide enough and whose tools are sharp enough for coping intelligently with alternative worldviews and for bringing balance and discernment to those fundamental issues on which every man must perforce take a stand and be answerable for the stand that he takes.[8]

Father Karl Rahner stresses the role of philosophy in one's personal formation:

[7]*The Documents of Vatican II, op. cit.*, pp. 444-45.
[8]R. O. Johann, S.J., "Philosophy in the Curriculum," in J. M. Lee and L. J. Putz, Eds., *Seminary Education in a Time of Change* (Notre Dame, Ind.: Fides, 1965), pp. 469, 476.

Only one who understands and autonomously masters himself can perceive that God's gift of himself in a personal revelation is an act of his free love. The philosopher who has a distinct, independent philosophy renders revelation possible.[9]

Self-mastery, mentioned by Fr. Rahner, is commended to the seminarian by Vatican Council II. No one without self-mastery is capable of love. Love is the gift of self. You cannot give what you do not possess. Self-possession is the meaning of habit (from the Latin *habere*: to possess). The seminarian attains self-mastery through the acquisition of habits, those various forms of self-possession which integrate one's personality under free will, to make the total gift of self in love and mercy.

Modern spiritual theology seeks its asceticism in the sacrifices demanded in the attainment and exercise of the virtues, in the sacrifices demanded by study and the works of mercy, by the apostolate and the missionary vocation of the Church. Asceticism looks beyond the individual, beyond the immediate community, to the world at large. In the words of Vatican II:

> The discipline required by seminary life should not be regarded merely as a strong support of community life and of charity. For it is a necessary part of the whole training program designed to provide self-mastery, to foster solid maturity of personality, and to develop other traits of character which are extremely serviceable for the ordered and productive activity of the Church.[10]

The life of grace will include the habit of using nature graciously, as a gift from God, gratefully accepted from him and lovingly given back to him, conformed to the

[9]Karl Rahner, S.J., "Philosophy and Theology," *Theology Digest*, St. Louis, 12 (Summer, 1964), 119-20.
[10]*The Documents of Vatican II, op. cit.*, p. 448.

image of Christ. Ascetical practices in the seminary should bring to fulfillment the sacramental characters of Baptism and Confirmation in preparation for the sacramental character of Holy Orders. St. Paul draws an analogy to the exercises of the athlete, which should not merely punish him, but make a positive contribution to his ability and eagerness to perform. Punishment is involved, to be sure. Modern track coaches have compared punishment to the sound barrier which one must penetrate if he is to attain maximum speeds. The athlete who grits his determination and makes heroic demands of himself just when he thinks he can run no faster, is able to break the sound barrier and run the mile in less than four minutes. The seminarian who makes similar demands of himself in the life of study and virtue finds that he can measure up to the heroic dimensions of Christ the Priest.

Erik Erikson ascribes mental troubles to this more than to any other cause: to what he calls "the repression of generativity," the repression of one's power and need to grow. The seminarian has dedicated his life to growth, to a "better, possible good." Though both the seminarian and his director have the common obligation of that better possible good, we may say that it is more the obligation of the director to make it possible, more the duty of the seminarian to make it better. As the seminarian makes his life better he increases his possibilities. The director, then, must be scouting for new possibilities. That is part of his executive role.

Zalesnik distinguishes two sorts of executive functions: the homeostatic, comparable to the healing process in medicine; the active, comparable to the processes of adaptation and growth. Executive functions may be sorted out along a passive-active continuum. Toward the passive end are those functions which seek to maintain the internal status quo of the organization. Toward the active end there are two kinds of executive function: the mediative, adjusting the organization internally in accord with changes in the environment; the proactive, seeking out new possibilities in the environment.[11]

What Father Flannery calls the "fortress mentality" was for too long influential in seminary policy. The consequence was an emphasis on those executive functions which lie toward the passive end of the continuum. The *aggiornamento* urged by Vatican II would stimulate creative thinking and greater emphasis upon the mediative and proactive functions.

[11]See A. Zalesnik, *Human Dilemmas of Leadership* (New York: Harper and Row, 1966), pp. 172 ff.

# 3: Psychological Testing

At any meeting where the formation of seminarians is dealt with, the subject of psychological testing invariably arises, whether in formal papers or in informal discussion. Upon hearing the claims made by many proponents of testing, the seminary director may well ask himself the question: Can there be a relaxation of efforts to perfect traditional means of personality testing, in expectation of a dramatic substitute from contemporary psychology or psychiatry? The answer is simple and straightforward: Those of professional competence within these latter disciplines tend to have no such expectations. At best, tests will supplement but not supplant traditional methods. The best judge of a seminarian's personality will remain the seminary director who has a thorough knowledge of the demands of seminary life.

## COMPETENCE OF TESTS

The average seminary director probably does not understand the technicalities of psychological testing, but he will be able to appreciate the weight of evidence represented in a review of opinions expressed by eminent authorities in the field. They have expressed themselves in readily understandable language.

Professor P. E. Vernon of the University of London has written:

> For over thirty years I have been perturbed by the conflicting claims of clinically oriented psychologists on the one hand and psychometrically oriented psychologists on the other hand, and their criticisms of each other. Neither side, it would seem, has succeeded in providing acceptable and practicable methods of diagnosis which are consistently more accurate than the un-

sophisticated methods that we ordinarily use in understanding people in daily life.[1]

Vernon is reiterating a judgment which he had expressed in a somewhat earlier work:

> Now though I have been working in this field of personality, on and off, for twenty-five years I cannot honestly claim that I, or other psychologists, have made much progress in the practical task of assessing personality simply and accurately. We fully realize the importance of taking personality factors into account in guiding or selecting children and adults into suitable educational or vocational careers. But we are certainly not in a position to provide the teacher, the Youth Employment Officers, or the personnel official, with a straightforward battery of tests at all comparable to our tests of aptitudes and attainments.[2]

Richard Meili of the University of Bern in Switzerland, in summarizing the present status of the test situation, says:

> Somehow, the whole preoccupation with personality tests was based on the notion that we really could perceive and characterize people very well, and that all that was necessary was to find methods with which this perception could be accomplished even faster and safer without having to observe people very long in daily behavior. We assumed too much. This recognition has become more widespread and has resulted in efforts to work our way out of this impasse.[3]

Klopfer, a clinical psychologist, admits that it is often the high-flown language of the psychological report, rather than any actual information contained therein, which impresses persons such as seminary directors.

[1] P. E. Vernon, *Personality Assessment: A Critical Survey* (London: Methuen, 1964), p. vii.

[2] P. E. Vernon, "The Assessment of Personality," in P. Halmos and A. Iliffe, Eds., *Readings in General Psychology* (New York: Philosophical Library, 1959), p. 145.

[3] R. Meili, "Research in Personality Assessment," in H. David and J. Brengelmann, *Perspectives in Personality Research* (New York: Springer, 1960), pp. 347-48.

If interpretations are couched in sufficiently palatable terms, it is no trick at all to impress some people. The implication is that psychologists should be wary of being misled by compliments from their colleagues in other professions. Perhaps their acceptance of psychological reports is due mainly to the smooth verbal techniques employed and not to any accuracy of interpretation or meaningful communication of findings.[4]

Oscar Buros, publisher of the monumental Mental Measurement Yearbook, speaks in the same vein.

At present, no matter how poor a test may be, if it is nicely packaged and if it promises to do all sorts of things which no test can do, the test will find many gullible buyers. When we initiated critical test reviewing in the 1938 Yearbook, we had no idea how difficult it would be to discourage the use of poorly constructed tests of unknown validity. Even the better informed test users who finally become convinced that a widely used test has no validity after all are likely to rush to use a new instrument which promises far more than any good test can possibly deliver. Counselors, personnel directors, psychologists, and school administrators seem to have an unshakeable will to believe the exaggerated claims of test authors and publishers. If these test users were better informed regarding the merits and limitations of their testing instruments, they would probably be less happy and less successful in their work. The test user who has faith—however unjustified—can speak with confidence in interpreting test results and in making recommendations. The well-informed test user cannot do this; he knows that the best of our tests are still highly fallible instruments which are extremely difficult to interpret in individual cases. Consequently, he must interpret test results cautiously and with so many reservations that others wonder whether he really knows what he is talking about. Children, parents, teachers, and school administrators are likely to have a greater respect and admiration for a school counselor who interprets test results with confidence, even though his interpretations have no scientific justification. The same applies to psychologists and personnel directors. Highly-trained psychologists appear to be as gullible as the less well-trained school counselors. It pays to know only a little about testing; furthermore, it is much

[4]W. G. Klopfer, *The Psychological Report* (New York: Grune and Stratton, 1960), p. 14. Used by permission.

225

more fun for everyone concerned—the examiner, the examinee, and the examiner's employer.[5]

## Buros then goes on to add:

We realize that the preceding paragraph may seem out of place in a test bibliography. Nevertheless, we are permitting it to stand. It probably reflects our discouragement at the little progress which has been made toward using tests more intelligently since we first started to publish frankly critical test reviews in the 1938 Yearbook. It is difficult to allocate the blame for the lack of greater progress. We think, however, that the major blame rests with the test users. The better test publishers would like to make more moderate claims for their tests. Unfortunately, test buyers don't want tests which make only moderate claims. Consequently, even the best test publishers find themselves forced by competition to offer test users what they want. Bad usage of tests is probably more common than good usage. Must it always be this way? We are afraid so. Although we think that test users will enjoy administering and interpreting tests more if they do not read the reviews which the tests have received in the MMY's, we hope that they will turn in ever-increasing numbers to the MMY's and consider the reviews carefully. Some of the reviews are conflicting and some are not particularly good reviews. But on the whole, the reviews represent the best and most authoritative source of critical information about currently published tests. If at times some reviews seem hypercritical, keep in mind that we have reason to believe that for every reviewer who is overly critical there are at least ten reviewers who pull their punches in assessing a test. It is, of course, more pleasant and more profitable to speak well of the work of others.[6]

REVIEW OF TESTS

All the reviews in the Mental Measurement Yearbooks are signed. For each of the more important tests there is a series of independent reviews by a number of individual authors. The tendency of criticism to be softened when a review is signed, which Buros affirms, may be seen by

[5]O. K. Buros, *Tests in Print* (Highland Park, N.J.: Gryphon, 1961), pp. xxiii-xxiv.
[6]*Loc. cit.*

comparing the signed reviews of the *New York Times Book Review Section* with their counterparts in the *London Times Literary Supplement,* which has a policy of unsigned reviews. The fact that they are signed does, therefore, give added weight to the evaluations of personality tests to which we make reference.

George K. Bennett, president of the Psychological Corporation, writes:

> Over the past forty years a great number of self-descriptive inventories have been constructed and tried out. This reviewer is unable to recall a well-established instance of useful validity for this class of questionnaire against a criterion of occupational success. . . . The mumbo jumbo of allegedly sophisticated statistical procedures is no substitute for demonstrated validity.[7]

The Minnesota Multiphasic Personality Inventory is a questionnaire which has received wide attention as a screening device for prospective candidates for seminary life. About the MMPI Albert Ellis has this to say:

> It can confidently be stated that in the whole history of modern psychology there has been no other personality inventory on which so much theoretical and practical work has been done. In spite of this research activity, the question of just how valid a clinical instrument the MMPI is has still not been finally settled. . . . Its absolute validity remains in doubt. . . . The efficacy of its use for individual diagnosis still remains to be proved. . . . It is to be wondered whether the clinical psychologist who cannot, in equal or less time, get more pertinent, incisive and depth-centered "personality" material from a straightforward interview technique is worth his salt. . . . About its usefulness for individual clinical diagnosis the present reviewer, for one, is still far from enthusiastic.[8]

Another commonly used test is the Rorschach. Professor Eysenck reviewed the literature of the previous five years

[7]G. K. Bennett, in O. K. Buros, *The Fifth Mental Measurements Yearbook* (Highland Park, N.J.: Gryphon, 1959), pp. 90-91.
[8]A. Ellis, in *ibid.,* pp. 166-67.

with respect to the validity of the Rorschach in its various applications and summarized his findings in ten conclusions, each of which indicts the test. He then goes on to say:

> These conclusions are not in principle different from those obtained by other reviewers; thus Cronbach has stated, "The test has repeatedly failed as a predictor of practical criteria. . . . There is nothing in the literature to encourage reliance on Rorschach interpretations" (in *Annual Review of Psychology*, Vol. 7, 173). Similarly, Payne came to the conclusions that "there is no evidence that the test is of any practical use at the moment, either for describing personality or for predicting behaviour" and "there is no evidence that the Rorschach can be used to assess whether or not individuals are well or poorly adjusted" (*Revue de Psychologie Applique*, Vol. 5, 255). In addition to the damning evidence regarding the validity of the Rorschach, it should perhaps also be pointed out that studies of the reliabilities of different Rorschach scores have shown these to be very low indeed. On all the usual criteria, therefore, it must be concluded that the Rorschach has failed to establish its scientific or practical value. This is becoming more widely recognized, largely as a consequence of the improved standard of Rorschach research in recent years, which has given rise to many well-controlled and well-analyzed studies, the results of which have been uniformly negative.[9]

Still another commonly used test is the Thematic Apperception Test. Concerning this test, Jensen writes:

> The TAT is perhaps the least standardized of all psychological tests as regards administration, scoring, and interpretation. . . . Various studies indicate that the TAT has little if any validity as a clinical test.[10]

Leonard Eron reviews the test in essentially the same language:

> It should be clearly understood . . . that in none of the studies relating TAT behavior to overt behavior is the obtained

[9]H. J. Eysenck, in *ibid.*, p. 277.
[10]A. J. Jensen, in *ibid.*, pp. 310-12.

relationship ever high enough to permit prediction in individual cases with any degree of confidence.[11]

Concerning tests such as the Rorschach and the TAT, which are called projective tests, Laurence Siegel has this to say:

> One is tempted to wonder . . . who does the major share of projecting when projective inventories are interpreted. To what extent does the interpretation made by the evaluator reveal his own personality rather than that of the client?[12]

Samuel Beck, after calling the human personality "probably the most complex datum in nature," goes on to add:

> Let it be said at once and unequivocally that validation such as is sought in a laboratory experiment is not at present to be expected for whole personality findings, whether by the Rorschach test or by any other. We do not know what variables may be complicating the person's behavior and are not being reached by our available tests. Then there are the interactions of forces within the personality, interactions which play a major role in shaping the man or woman as known by others.[13]

Seminary directors should certainly not take a test more seriously than do members of the psychological profession. An example of the psychologist's attitude when speaking candidly to fellow professionals is seen in the remarks of Father John Stafford, C.S.V., then head of the Department of Psychology at The Catholic University of America:

> Many other things come and go. We go through these "phases" at our place, too. We had a Szondi workshop a few years ago and everybody got excited about doing Szondies. We had a rash of Szondi dissertations. Now we have a whole shelf full of Szondi books that nobody ever takes down. And

[11]L. D. Eron, in *ibid.*, p. 310.
[12]L. Siegel, in *ibid.*, p. 233.
[13]S. J. Beck, in *ibid.*, p. 275.

we also had Margaret Lowenfeld around for some days, and we went into a Mosaic "phase." We will play around with many things that come along, but frankly we take few of them very seriously.[14]

In 1950, as president of Columbia University, General Eisenhower inaugurated the Conservation of Human Resources Project. In cooperation with the Armed Forces, the Selective Service System, the Veterans Administration, various governmental agencies, and certain large corporations, a study was made of the records relating to the eighteen million men screened for service during World War II. Three volumes were published in 1959. The conclusion germane to our present consideration of testing was this:

> There is no way of finding out what a man can really do except by the slow and costly process of trying him out. . . . The individual's qualities can be properly appraised only as they are revealed in given situations, under given circumstances.[15]

The same conclusion has been drawn by Vernon:

> It is always worth remembering that a period of trial on an actual job is likely to be more predictive of future success at this job than any short-cut method.[16]

THE BEST JUDGE OF FITNESS

Given that the most reliable test of a seminarian's fitness is to let him live the life or to make inquiries about his behavior over prolonged periods of his earlier life, we may ask who is the most competent judge of his fitness. Here

---

[14]J. Stafford, "The University in Clinical Psychology," in M. Finn and F. Brown, Eds., *Training for Clinical Psychology* (New York: International Universities Press, 1959), p. 52.

[15]E. Ginzberg, *et al.*, *Patterns of Performance* (3 vols.) (New York: Columbia University Press, 1959), pp. 276, 272-73.

[16]Vernon, *Personality Assessment: A Critical Survey, op. cit.*, p. 265.

again we find contemporary psychologists making candid admissions. Cronbach, for instance, writes:

> There is no evidence that psychological training gives the observer an advantage. . . . The clinician's experience and theoretical background gives him confidence in the judgments he makes, but seems not to make his judgments actually superior to those of the intelligent untrained observer who knows the job requirements. . . . The most important requirement for valid assessment is that the assessor have a clear understanding of the psychological requirements of the criterion task.[17]

This is also the opinion of Thorne, who says:

> Continuous observation yields data which cannot be obtained from single interviews or test procedures. . . . It is difficult to create laboratory or test situations which will sample the extreme of healthy vs. unhealthy behavior. . . . Ideally, such behavior ratings should be made by trained observers who have actually seen the person in action. Practically, the information may be obtained from parents, relatives, teachers, ward personnel, or other persons who have information about the person.
>
> Laymen often make quite astute estimates of personality and intelligence. In fact it remains to be demonstrated whether professional psychologists consistently average more valid estimates of personality than a "natural" leader who has shown high ability to "size up" people. . . . Laymen may not be able to differentiate or communicate the cues upon which their discriminations are based, but it is apparently not too difficult to learn such skills intuitively. Many laymen approach the problem validly by formulating commonsense questions to which intuitive answers can be reached. . . .
>
> It appears that the psychologically unsophisticated layman acquires the ability to make value judgments due to factors of native intelligence and experience in much the same manner as vocabulary is acquired more or less spontaneously and effortlessly and is thereby regarded as a good index of intelligence level. . . . All this has been accomplished in the past without the benefit of formal test procedures, and it has yet to be determined whether test procedures can produce more

[17] L. J. Cronbach, *Essentials of Psychological Testing* (second edition; New York: Harper and Row, 1960), p. 589.

valid or efficient judgment than can competent clinical judgment.[18]

The seminary director can have confidence in his ability to assess the personality of those in his charge. Professor Vernon affirms this in much the same language as that of Thorne and Cronbach:

> The remarkable facility we have for judging people's motives and traits in everyday social intercourse or in interviews . . . the processes involved are essentially the same as those involved in perception of the physical world. The clinical psychologist or psychiatrist, with his more sophisticated knowledge of human motives derived from Freudian or depth psychology, should be capable of more accurate diagnoses of, and predictions about, people; but this is not borne out by the experimental evidence.[19]

There is no magic in psychology or psychiatry, anymore than elsewhere. Seminary directors cannot be relieved of the unglamorous workaday methods of assessing the personality and progress of seminarians. What Professor Meili has said will continue to hold:

> Since we are above all supposed to perceive people relative to their daily behavior, it is essential to pay more attention to this area. Methodologically, it is much more difficult to study daily life behavior than to work with tests; and the questionnaires are hardly a dependable aid in overcoming these difficulties. But, experiments made on the basis of direct observations indicate that this method is more valuable than many tests.[20]

There is an extensive ongoing effort to develop psychological tests of seminarians which might augment the observational and judgmental abilities of the director who

---

[18]F. C. Thorne, *Principles of Psychological Examining* (Brandon, Vt.: Journal of Clinical Psychology, 1955), pp. 162-63.
[19]Vernon, *Personality Assessment: A Critical Survey, op. cit.,* p. vii.
[20]Meili, *op. cit.,* p. 355.

must make the final evaluation. The sentiments of research workers are fairly expressed in the following paragraphs, co-authored by a psychiatrist and a psychologist:

> Each method of assessment has its own peculiar advantages and weaknesses. Taken as a whole, the available methods of judging a human being—both primitive and their modern counterparts—are grossly inadequate to the job, and always will be. We can conceive of no magic method that will accurately reflect the infinite complexities of the human personality, its variegated nuances, fathomless depths, or unpredictability in new situations. Most critics of psychological methodology expect too much. Most defenders of this methodology promise too much. The human being with over nine billion unpredictable cortical synapses defies predictable adherence to any known laws. Yet, we must somehow deal with this colossus—the human personality—if we are to have any kind of a science of behavior. We certainly cannot give up before we start. Neither can we admit failure because success is not always complete.
>
> Over and over we hear the accusation that psychological tests are inadequate. These accusations do not only come from the man on the street, who resents "playing with blocks" as an insult to his maturity, but also from professional persons, from psychologists, from professors of psychology, and even from those who earn their living by using and selling tests. Article after article in the professional literature point out how this or that test has failed to live up to expectations. When one hears this criticism over a long enough period of time, one is, at last, tempted to agree—yes, phychological tests are no good. But then comes the question—where do we go from here?[21]

Seminary directors will, indeed, wish to collaborate in present efforts to develop a testing program for use at the seminary level. But the fruits of such efforts will be largely at the research level for the foreseeable future. The judgment of the seminary director will continue to be the primary means of personality assessment. The ways in which his

---

[21]T. C. Kahn and M. B. Giffen, *Psychological Techniques in Diagnosis and Evaluation* (New York: Pergamon, 1960), p. 9.

judgment can be supplemented by tests in their present form is explained by Vernon and other authors, such as those to whose works we have made reference.[22]

In a way the seminary director is like a judge in a court of law: obliged to make decisions which affect the destiny of the human individual in a profound way. As with the judge, the fairmindedness of the seminary director forces him to look to psychology for all the help he can get. Concerning the help available from psychology, Wigmore, a recognized master in the area of legal evidence, writes:

> Judicial practice is entitled and bound to resort to all *truths of human nature established by science*, and to employ *all methods recognized by scientists* for applying those truths in the analysis of testimonial credit. Already, in long tradition, judicial practice is based on the implicit recognition . . . of a number of principles of testimonial psychology, empirically discovered and accepted. Insofar as science from time to time revises them, or adds new ones, the law can and should recognize them. Indeed, it may be asserted that the courts are ready to learn and to use, whenever the psychologists produce it, any method which the latter themselves are agreed is sound, accurate, and practical. If there is any reproach, it does not belong to the courts or the law. A legal practice which has admitted the evidential use of the telephone, the phonograph, the dictograph, and the vacuum-ray, within the past decades, cannot be charged with lagging behind science. But where *are* these practical psychological tests, which will detect specifically the memory failure and the lie on the witness stand? There must first be proof of general scientific recognition that they are valid and feasible. The vacuum-ray photographic method, for example, was accepted by scientists the world over, within a few months after its promulgation. If there is ever devised a psychological test for the valuation of witnesses, the law will run to meet it. Both law and practice permit the calling of any expert scientist whose method is acknowledged in his science to be a sound and trustworthy one. Whenever the

[22]See R. J. Menges and J. E. Dittes, *Psychological Studies of Clergymen: Abstracts of Research* (New York: Nelson, 1965).

psychologist is really ready for the courts, the courts are ready for him.[23]

Whenever the psychologist is ready for the seminary, the seminary is ready for him.

While awaiting further help from psychology and offering his own collaboration toward that end, the director must decide what seminary life demands of a person and observe how well the seminarian measures up to that demand in day to day living. I will give two examples of what famous psychologists have looked for under such circumstances. John B. Watson wrote:

> Once I had to write a little brief on the chief factors in judging men for jobs. I wrote that if I had to select an individual on the basis of any one characteristic, I should choose work habits—actual love of work, willingness to take an overload of work, to work longer than actual specified hours, and to clean the chips up after the work is done. These things, I find, have to be drilled into the individual pretty early or he will never get them. No psychological test so far devised will bring out the strength or weakness of the individual in these particulars.[24]

Ernest Jones, colleague and biographer of Freud, gave the indications which he sought in assessing a personality:

> We surmise that the psychological problem of normality must ultimately reside in the capacity to endure—in the ability to hold wishes in suspension without either renouncing them or "reacting" to them in defensive ways. Freedom and self-control are thus seen to be really the same thing, though both are badly misused concepts. We reach the conclusion that the nearest attainable criterion of normality is fearlessness. The most

---

[23] J. A. Wigmore, *Evidence in Trials at Common Law* (Boston: Little, Brown, 1940), III, pp. 367-68.

[24] J. B. Watson, "Assessing Personality," in *Psychology: A Course of Readings* (London: International University Society, 1957), p. 247.

normal person is, like Siegfried, *angstfrei*, but we must be clear that we mean by this not merely manifest courage, but the absence of all the deep reactions that mask unconscious apprehensiveness. Where these are absent we have the willing or even joyful acceptance of life, with all its visitations and chances, that distinguishes the free personality of one who is master of himself.[25]

The seminarian should be able to say with Mary: "Behold the servant of the Lord. Be it done unto me according to thy word." He should have the courage to face his future without having it spelled out beforehand, and the faith to have it spelled out in due time by God and his Church.

[25]E. Jones, "The Concept of a Normal Mind," in Halmos and Iliffe, *op. cit.*, p. 355.